Hey Suburbia is published under Erudition Books, sectionalized division under Di Angelo Publications INC.

ERUDITION BOOKS

an imprint of Di Angelo Publications. Hey Suburbia Copyright 2021 Mike Damante in digital and print distribution in the United States of America.

Library of congress cataloging-in-publications data

Hey Suburbia downloadable via Kindle, iBooks and NOOK.

Library of Congress Registration Paperback

ISBN: 9781942549772

Cover and Interior Illustrations: Cassie Podish
Words and Photos: Mike Damante
Interior Design: Kimberly James

No part of this book may be copied or distributed without the publisher's written approval. For educational, business and bulk orders, contact sales@diangelopublications.com.

1. Music -- Essays
2. Music -- Genres & Styles -- Punk
3. Music -- Philosophy & Social Aspects
4. Music -- History & Criticism
United States of America with int.   distribution

HEY SUBURBIA

A GUIDE TO THE EMO/POP PUNK RISE

MIKE DAMANTE

ART BY **CASSIE PODISH**

ACKNOWLEDGEMENTS

I'd like to thank my wife, family, and friends. Thanks to Elizabeth, Sequoia, and Cassie. Thanks to Michele Stephens, Matt Pryor, Erik Stein, The X-Games, Vans Warped Tour press staff, Epitaph Records, weworemasks.com (RIP), Jeff "Rhino" Neumann, Scott Heisel, Rick Devoe, Todd Spoth Photography, Andrew Youngblood, Bethany Watson, Zach / Jamie (and Ava), Billy Martin, The Dirt (222,) Riot Fest, Jenni Weinman, Gavin Caswell, Kevin Bivona, To The Stars/AC, Shawna Potter, Jamie Espinosa, Chris No. 2, Becky Kovach, Mike Cubillos, Dayna Ghiraldi, Matt Skiba, Macbeth, Tom DeLonge, The Daily Cougar, Houston Chronicle, Vagrant Records, Dylan Anderson/Hi My Name Is Mark, Mariel Loveland, Chris Farren, South by Southwest, Fat Tony, Saves The Tuesday, and you.

INTRODUCTION: HEY, YOU'RE PART OF IT	8
LOS ANGELES IS BURNING	15
SECOND WAVE SERENADE	18
KNOW YOUR ROOTS	29
I HATE THIS TOWN	34
YOU'RE NOT PUNK AND I'M TELLING EVERYONE	40
I WANT TO BE STEREOTYPED. I WANT TO BE CLASSIFIED.	46
THIS SONG WILL BECOME THE ANTHEM OF YOUR UNDERGROUND	51
I GUESS THIS IS GROWING UP	56
SAVE YOUR GENERATION	63
THE PAST IS ONLY THE FUTURE WITH THE LIGHTS ON	73
EMO ISN'T A FOUR-LETTER WORD	80
WHEN I GOT THE MUSIC I GOT A PLACE TO GO	85
A NEW AMERICANA	88
THE FUTURE FREAKS ME OUT	92
NEW NOISE	95
SCENE REPORT: ARTISTS, PUBLICISTS AND INDUSTRY FOLK'S BEST MEMORIES	97

TABLE OF CONTENTS

A DAY IN THE LIFE OF A TOUR MANAGER	106
ULTIMATE PLAYLIST	112
TOP PUNK SONGS OF THE ERA	122
FILM GUIDE	126
TOP COMPLIATIONS	128
GLOSSARY	130
ESSENTIAL ALBUMS	134
ABOUT THE AUTHOR	148
ABOUT THE ARTIST	150

"HEY YOU'RE PART OF IT"

I heard this comment often as a young adult. I was a music journalist for a local outlet, meeting and interviewing my childhood idols, yet the film never resonated with me.

The punk scene was a different breed; it was void of the traditional rock star attitudes, no matter how big the band was. I never really saw the artists on a celebrity pedestal. They remained accessible, greetings fans at the merch table or outside the venue after the show.

Once, a line of kids wrapped around the parking lot trailing from Social Distortion's tour bus. The high schoolers and pre-teens were waiting to meet the legendary front man Mike Ness. Even being an elder statesman in punk, and being older than his counterparts, Ness came out and greeted every fan. He took photos, signed autographs, and talked with fans. He didn't *have* to do that, but he did.

From the start, the leaders of the scene were incredibly down to Earth, and punk fans emulated their behavior. I witnessed this personally time and time again. Once, when I was a student journalist at the Universityof Houston, I went to a local Angels & Airwaves concert. When I was leaving the venue, I ran into the guitar tech. We just started talking and he noticed my Angels & Airwaves tattoo, and told me to wait right there.

I didn't ask for anything, but within minutes he was handing me a VIP pass and escorting me backstage. For many, blink-182 was that gateway drug for punk and **pop-punk**, and I grew up worshipping that band. Tom DeLonge of blink-182 fronted Angels & Airwaves after blink's first **indefinite hiatus**. Ryan Sinn, of the Distillers fame, was playing bass at the time. Sinn came up to me and took me back to meet rest of the band. As DeLonge approached, the first thing he did was look at my arm and comment on my "rad" Alkaline Trio tattoo. I was surprised he noticed that one first instead of the Angels & Airwaves one, or the blink-182 classic bunny.

You've heard the phrase "never meet your heroes," but that wasn't the case with this experience. Later on, I was sitting on a couch with his manager Rick DeVoe, and DeLonge started to randomly air drum to entertain us. He didn't have to amuse us; being mere feet from one of my idols was captivating enough.

At the time, I was at community college getting my basics done but I was headfirst into the pop-punk/punk and emo scenes. My bedroom wall was adorned with stickers, posters and show fliers. My love for the genre started in high school, as 1990s alt-rock was always on repeat, as well as with punk and ska acts blink-182, The Mighty Mighty Bosstones, and Rancid. My wardrobe was band T-shirts, and baggy skate shorts. I was going to shows constantly; I met one of my best friends in the pit of a Bouncing Souls show by intervening when some jock tried to go after him.

Music was life.

I got into journalism at my high school. I wrote for the school newspaper, and my senior year I was co-sports editor, and I loved it. I was enthralled by the process of journalism; the methods of seeking truth, interviewing, and constructing well-rounded and balanced stories.

Once I started taking the concept of higher education seriously and transferred from a community college to a university, well, that is when my love for journalism really took off. There was an Advanced Reporting class I was taking in the Communications college at the University of Houston. The class was basically working for the school paper *The Daily Cougar*, which at the time was technically the second daily in town next to the *Houston Chronicle*. I was given the beat of technology, which really honed my news writing skills, but to bulk up my portfolio I started to write for the Life and Arts sections almost religiously. I was churning out around ten articles a week. I would review albums, movies, and do news and sports stories on campus. Life and Arts gave me the outlet to write about the music and bands I loved. I noticed since college kids were the key demographic for a lot of artists, labels and publicists would constantly send us CDs, advance downloads, and other promo materials. The labels and PR teams were also very gracious with granting us interviews; the first band I ever interviewed was Story Of The Year for *The Daily Cougar*.

Another class I enjoyed was copy editing. The teacher was also an editor at the *Houston Chronicle*. There was something about him that was admirable; he commanded respect and was the type of guy you wanted to work hard for and impress. I never imagined that doing well in his class would lead to a gig at the *Houston Chronicle*, but it did. I started out small. I would go to class till about 3 p.m. every day, work at the school paper during lunch and after school, and then go copy edit at the *Houston Chronicle* until 1 a.m. It was a grind, and I was hooked. This continued after graduation, as I stayed on at the *Chronicle* as a copy editor and web producer, and convinced the features editors to let me write about music whenever the opportunity presented itself.

Now, I'm not some famous "scene" music journalist like Scott Heisel or Dan Ozzi. So why is this book important?

I'd like to consider myself somewhat of an authority on the pop-punk genre. Despite not always having the support or promotion of the publication, I covered the specific music scene intensely for a top-four market. I've attended countless shows, covered ten **Warped Tours**, and have interviewed, or at least met, anyone you could imagine from the pop-punk/emo era. I have endless stories (some will be shared throughout this book), but ultimately, what moved me to write this book was because I feel *part* of something. Even when I wasn't writing about shows or bands, the underdog mentality and punk rock ethos was still a part of me.

I felt compelled to start chronicling the scene years ago, as "emo nights" started to become a trend in many major U.S. cities. I never stopped listening to any of these bands or going to shows even after leaving the *Chronicle*.

The quotes included in this book are from interviews I conducted over the years covering this style of music. This isn't the be-all-tell-all authority on the scene or a full historical account.

Hey Suburbia is more of a look back at the rise of a musical movement, exploring why it was pivotal punks and outcasts alike. This isn't a traditional book in the sense of structure. This book took many incarnations before finally becoming a reality.

If anything, I hope this book serves as a reminder that, sometimes, nostalgia isn't just about the past, but how those precious moments in time empower the present and fuel the future. Consider this a love letter to one of the greatest time periods of our lives.

LOS ANGELES IS BURNING

Punk broke into the mainstream in the 1990s, with Green Day at the front of the **punk-rock** pack, which included an influx of California talent like Rancid, Offspring and Bad Religion. Punk returning to the radio paved the way for a second coming of sorts, as the genre had remained mostly underground since the heyday of The Clash and Ramones. Fresh off Green Day's success, blink-182's pop-punk prowess in 1999 helped launch pop-punk back into the mainstream with a vengeance. Major labels were signing up bands left and right, indie labels like **Drive Thru Records** and its acts were all over the scene, and bands like Good Charlotte and Simple Plan became household names.

While many bands that came out of this trend were horrible, the 2000s era propelled the careers of acts like New Found Glory and Alkaline Trio, while also reinvigorating older acts like MxPx and Less Than Jake. Although the trend died down in pop culture, the bands didn't and neither did the music. "Pop Punk's Not Dead" was a slogan New Found Glory adopted, playing off of the "Punk's Not Dead" phrase many punk fans uttered years after The Ramones and The Clash were gone.

Today, most of these bands are still kicking, and even their punk rock predecessors are hanging around. It is more than just nostalgia; this movement in music was not merely the major labels' flavor of the month. Far from a fad, the emo and pop-punk era remains fundamental to the fans who grew up singing along to The Used, and stitching together their broken hearts to Dashboard Confessional. "Emo nights" are in every major city in the United States; the bands are still earning a nice living playing to capacity crowds of concert-goers new and old.

There may be more facial hair, faded ink, and families back home, but the scene is alive. It never died or went anywhere, but the recent revival proves that pop-punk isn't dead, and never really was.

SECOND WAVE SERENADE

"SOUTHERN CALIFORNIA'S BREEDING MOMMY'S LITTLE MONSTER"

In the 1990s, the landscape of rock music changed with Nirvana ushering in a grunge element to alternative rock, which opened the doors for bands like Pearl Jam and Soundgarden. This edgier style of rock helped make the genre more appealing to the masses. The 1990s saw the rise of many alt-rock acts like Smashing Pumpkins, Bush, Hole, Third Eye Blind, Eve 6, Everclear, Foo Fighters, Garbage, and many others. With rock music becoming just as prevalent as pop, already-big bands like Metallica were able to grow their audiences even more.

If you look at the roots of rock trends throughout the years, you could point to the 90s being a pivotal turning point for music in general. Nirvana's ascension set the scene for what would later become an explosion of raw music.

The pop-punk/**emo** craze of the late 1990s and early 2000s was just as important to some as the first-wave punk, goth and grunge eras. The scene expanded from the Warped Tour to the world; Allister went from playing the Chicago suburbs to the biggest cities in Japan.

Punk rock had its first flirtation with the masses through genre originators The Ramones, Sex Pistols and The Clash, who all saw success in the late 1970s and early 1980s. In 1994, Green Day, the Offspring, and the **Epitaph Records** roster ushered punk rock back to the mainstream and took to heights that were taller than any punk's liberty spikes.

Green Day hit at a perfect time; MTV was dominated by grunge bands, upbeat 90s alt-rock and other "buzzworthy" sounding bands. Green Day's *Dookie* perfectly bridged the gap between the alternative rock and punk worlds, and their music videos weren't out of place next to Nirvana's. The Offspring was another band that produced alt-rock heavy punk, and their record sales soared.

No Doubt, a small Orange County **ska**-tinged act, put out one of the biggestalternative rock records of all time: *Tragic Kingdom*. With over 16 million copies sold, the album pushed the band, and Gwen Stefani, to superstardom.

The success of those bands made the music world take notice, and record sales started pouring in for Rancid, Bad Religion, Pennywise, NOFX and others. Soon, Southern California became the breeding ground for melodic punk, and helped put that region of America on the sonic map. Indie labels like Epitaph and **Fat Wreck Chords** were now giving the majors a run for their money. The Offspring's *Smash* was certified six-times platinum. The early success of NOFX's records allowed Fat Mike to build Fat Wreck

Chords as an indie empire in NOFX's image.

With radio play and catchy songs, it was easy to consider Green Day as one of the pop-punk pioneers. The songs were still snotty and sweaty, but accessible enough to attract jocks and cheerleaders to the shows. Green Day's Lookout! Records discography is full East Bay-influenced Ramones-core, and *Dookie*, while slightly slowed down, still had enough edge to make the pop-punk tag okay for Green Day.

Similar to how Green Day, The Offspring, and Rancid brought the early 90s punk revival to the top of alternative rock, blink-182 took **skate-punk** to the masses in 1999 with *Enema of the State*. The album introduced a new wave of youth to catchy, angst-driven music, and opened up doors for bands, new and old, to reach radio. Blink-182 had seen major label success beforehand, with 1997's seminal fan favorite *Dude Ranch*, with "Dammit" and "Josie" being big skate punk songs and 1990s alt-rock singles.

But with *Enema of the State*, they became MTV mainstays. As they became more popular, going from the Warped Tour to **TRL**, fickle punk police deemed them sellouts. They judged the album by its three pop-leaning singles ("What's My Age Again," "All The Small Things" and "Adam's Song"). Green

Day faced similar backlash when they hit it big, too.

Major companies were scouting skate parks, pop-punk bands were being signed as the next big thing, and bands wanted to replicate blink's crossover success. Joel and Benji Madden went from poverty to celebrity with Good Charlotte. Sum 41 was sandwiched between Nelly and Christina Aguilera videos on MTV. Labels like Drive Thru Records and Vagrant suddenly became big players. The indie labels became a breeding ground for executives looking to hit lightning with a Mest or a Sugarcult.

You also had indie labels acting like major labels with iron-clad contracts and a corporate mentality aimed at profiting at the expense of the artist. Victory Records started with some of the scene's brightest young bands like Taking Back Sunday, Hawthorne Heights, and Thursday before eventually targeting many heavier-sounding bands. But with growth of the musical scenes, came new problems.

The label was sued by three separate artists (Streetlight Manifesto, A Day to Remember, and Hawthorne Heights), and the bands Thursday and Aiden were both vocal with issues they had with Victory about financial compensation, including royalties.

Bands alleged the environment at Victory was mafia-like, stating label president Tony Brummel offered hookers in the office.

Platinum selling pop-punk came into existence duringthe dying days of the boy band trend. Itmingled with TRL acts and the rise of nu-metal (Korn,Limp Bizkit) and Britney Spears. It wasn't uncommon to hear Eminem and Jimmy Eat World on your local pop-radio station. New Found Glory was no longer just a fan of what was on the radio, they were station hits themselves.

"I remember listening to the radio on the way home from school," said Mariel Loveland from Candy Hearts/Best-Ex. "And for months I was listening to this Top 40 station and trying to tape this song on cassette, and it was New Found Glory 'My Friends Over You.' That was literally the only CD I listened to for like a year."

The music was upbeat, sugary, and tailor-made for radio. While the subject matter was serious, and at times sad, there wasn't the anger and vitriol that fueled traditional punk music. As the George Bush presidential years approached, the music started to reflect the changing political and societal climate. Fat Mike's voter-drive effort Punk Voter recruited the support of popular bands like blink-182,

Yellowcard, Alkaline Trio and others. Tom DeLonge even campaigned with Democratic challenger John Kerry. This turbulent time period led to Green Day's *American Idiot*, which was rich in political undertones all wrapped up in a modern-day rock opera.

The pop-punk/emo craze couldn't have come at a better time. The radio airwaves and MTV were oversaturated with commercial pop music. The youth wanted something heartfelt that spoke directly to them and their emotions. Emotive music wasn't anything new, and you can certainly argue any musical genre can incite passion, but the songs written by these bands struck the right chords at the perfect time.

"So much of that time period is a blur because a lot was happening so fast for us," said Good Charlotte's Billy Martin. "It's one of those things that you have to reflect on after the fact because you are so in the moment. It's hard to realize. MTV and TRL specifically were super popular at the time, and they were major platforms for artists. When our debut album came out, it was at a time where boybands and pop stars were ruling the charts. There was also a push from the other side where heavy bands like Korn and Limp Bizkit were killing it too. I think we came along at a perfect time for MTV because we wrote pop songs, but we played our own instruments and we were a real band. It kind of married what was happening on MTV at the time. I think a lot of success in this industry is timing."

For the male-dominated bands, men were allowed to be emotional again. The bravado and machismo that infested nu metal and corporate radio rock was replaced by sensitivity, and vulnerability, which in part lent to popularity of these artists. The emotional accessibility and raw realness of the lyrics, combined with the delivery and overall presentation, made it feel more authentic than what radio was previously pandering to.

"When I first started playing guitar, there weren't very many women playing rock in the mainstream," said Loveland. "I could look at the Thermals, Tegan and Sara, or someone like Jenny Lewis, but role models were scarce, and those bands certainly didn't exist in the same world as Warped Tour. Even a decade later, I found myself as one of the lone women sleeping in a tour bus with all men, fielding comments about how my butt looks in pajamas. On the other side, I watched so many of the other talented women around me step on each other to get ahead, or cut each other down. It felt like they truly believed there was only space for one of us, which isn't something I ever subscribed to. As a result, I often felt like I had no place anywhere but with the people in my band."

Though the competition was intense, these weren't your traditional rock stars in the sense of over-the-top show production, diva-like behavior and overall attitude. The down-to-earth elements of these bands were another selling point; the person next door playing his or her guitar too loud could be the next big thing. The appeal reached record label executives, fans, and anyone who casually saw the way the bands were presented.

It was a mutually beneficial relationship for all parties involved. The labels were able to capitalize off the trend. For the fans, they got greater accessibility to the band's music and merchandise, and were able to foster a closer connection to the music and the people making it. The bands were able to prosper as well. Melodic **hard core** act H20 was signed up by a major label, and released just one record, *Go!,* with MCA Records, who were known for blink-182 and Fenix TX. Signing deals were common at the time, and with the money from *Go!,* H20's front man Toby Morse was able to buy a house in Los Angeles. Now, with the music industry's changing landscape, and streaming services, this scenario is almost unheard of.

Green Day raked in the green during its time (and truly never stopped being a money machine). Good Charlotte sold about 3.5 million copies of *The Young and the Hopeless*. Blink-182's *Enema of the State* sold over 15 million records. The success of these records led to other like-sounding acts achieving similar success. Yellowcard's "Ocean Avenue" moved 1 million units, and Fall Out Boy's *From Under The Cork Tree* sold around 3.5 million and pushed them to the eventual next big thing.

In the 1990s, the third wave of ska music hit the mainstream with acts like The Mighty Mighty Bosstones, Reel Big Fish, No Doubt, Goldfinger and others finding a way to get on radio and MTV. There were also bands like Less Than Jake that saw benefits from both booms: the ska and the pop-punk craze in the early 2000s.

"We were the Reese's candy of the scene," Chris DeMakes of Less Than Jake said. "Instead of the perfect melding of chocolate and peanut butter, we were the perfect blend of punk rock and ska. We benefitted quite well from that when those two scenes simultaneously exploded."

There were also cross-promotional opportunities that didn't exist before. Restaurant chain Denny's partnered with bands to make signature meals inspired by them. Some of the dishes included Sum 41's "The Sumwich," Good Charlotte's "Band of Burritos," and Gym Class Heroes' "After School

Special." The All-American Rejects, The Plain White T's, Taking Back Sunday, and Girls Like Boys also had dishes alongside larger acts like Katy Perry, Rascal Flatts and Los Lonely Boys.

The bands became accidental rock stars, and heartthrobs overnight. There's always a fine line between band and celebrity, and the status of some of these bands would be altered. You'd soon see Good Charlotte on the same red carpet as Jay-Z and Diddy. How weird was it to see the guys from Sum 41 in teen magazines?

"When we started, all we wanted to do was tour and not work normal jobs," said Adam Lazzara of Taking Back Sunday, speaking on *Tell All Your Friends'* success. "The way everything kind of progressed was awesome."

KNOW YOUR ROOTS

Punk rock always had a regional taste before the invention of the Internet. Northern California had the East Bay bands like Rancid, Green Day, Jawbreaker and Operation Ivy. Southern California gave birth to the Descendents, NOFX, Pennywise, Bad Religion and a punk rock sound that helped define the Epitaph and Fat Wreck Chords roster for years. The unique sound would heavily influence the future of pop-punk. Even some of the punker bands from that region still churned out some of the catchiest songs. The Descendents sang about girls, food and farts, perfectly blending the spirit of the Beach Boys with "Blitzkrieg Bop," which helped birth the blink-182s and MxPxs of the world.

Bad Religion, while influenced by early D.C. hard core, wrote harmonies and soaring choruses that made the whole scene rethink how punk music was written. Bad Religion also added an intellectual element to punk; you feel equally angsty and empowered as Greg Graffin (PHD, author, professor) used diction like *jurisprudence*, and sung lyrics like "Puritan work ethic maintains its subconscious edge as Old Glory maintains your consciousness" (from "You Are The Government").

NOFX helped create skate punk, and the whole Fat Wreck sound that led to No Use For A Name and Lagwagon. The songs were all similar tempos, and the sense of humor and self-awareness followed. The on-stage banter of Fat Mike, Eric Melvin and El Hefe introduced a comedy element to the stage show, but the band was never a joke. NOFX's on-stage antics were also copied by younger bands like blink-182 and Sum 41. NOFX will go down as one of the biggest independent punk bands, and one of the most important American punk bands.

Hot Water Music's southern-fried punk rock led to Against Me! and the Gainesville gruffy sound. The Fest is one of the biggest punk festivals in the Southern United States that brings in concert goers from all over the country to see smaller acts side-by-side with headliners like Jawbreaker and Lagwagon.

The Chicago scene started with Screeching Weasel and Naked Raygun, and led to the likes of Alkaline Trio, The Plain White T's, Allister, Mest, Rise Against, and eventually Fall Out Boy. Arguably, one of the best festivals in all of music emanates from Chicago, and is a celebration of a who's who with Riot Fest. Riot Fest usually bucks the common festival circuit trends that other large festivals do in putting homogenous lineups together by knowing their audience, and smartly booking acts that will attract the casual festival fan as well. Riot Fest was able to book legendary legacy acts like the original Misfits, The Replacements, and Jawbreaker for headlining reunion sets at Riot Fest. The festival also pushed having bands play fan-favorite records in its entirety as another selling point for the tour, which in punk rock ethos has always kept ticket prices affordable. The 2019 Riot Fest had single-day tickets as low as $49.99.

The East Coast had New York hard core like H20, but in the shadow of the CBGB, the surrounding areas and neighboring states started their own sound. New Jersey would someday give birth to upbeat punk like the Bouncing Souls and pop-punk/emo acts like Lifetime and Saves The Day, emo rockers My Chemical Romance, and rock'n' roll revivalists The Gaslight Anthem. A post-hardcore Long Island sound led to Taking Back Sunday, Brand New, and the Movielife.

It wasn't just an American institution; it was a global domination. Canadian acts Sum 41, Simple Plan, Gob, Chixdiggit, Reset, and Propagandhi all came from north of the border. Canadian pop-star Avril Lavigne even borrowed from some of the pop-punk trend with her fashion sense, and songs like "Complicated" and "Sk8er Boi."

The skate-park sounds reached across the Atlantic Ocean with Sweden's Millencolin becoming a go-to for skate soundtracks, and acts like Israel's Useless I.D. signing to Fat Wreck Chords.

Of course, the coasts would all influence each other, as New Found Glory sounded more like Los Angeles than Orlando. A melting pot would be created from punk, pop-punk, post-hardcore, and emo from each region's unique history. All these bands and regions were huge parts in crafting the scene's present sound and future.

"Before I go on stage with whatever I do with any of my bands or whatever, I always have this specific hour where I blast and listen to old punk rock music that I listened to in junior high and high school," said Tom DeLonge of blink-182, Box Car Racer and Angels & Airwaves. "When I listen to those old punk bands it gets me excited because the whole idea is that it makes me feel the way I felt when I started playing guitar, and my whole reason for wanting to break out of suburbia and do something bigger."

I HATE THIS TOWN

"AT THE RIGHT PLACE AT THE RIGHT TIME"

A common theme in pop-punk songs then and now was a way to "get out of this town." For many bands, music became more than just an escape from a small-town life, it became a career. Some fizzled out, some stayed the course, some bands made a profession, and others had moderate musical success.

Fenix TX hopped right on the pop-punk train, venturing from Houston to San Diego, being plucked from Drive Thru by major label MCA along the way. Despite being on MTV and on movie soundtracks, Fenix TX didn't get Texas-sized love, but they were hits in California.

"I felt like we never got the response in our hometown," said Adam Lewis of Fenix TX. "We were getting played on KROQ but not [Houston]."

For any band playing the style of music during this period, there was a larger talent pool for labels to look for locally. So many kids were forming garage bands and bands were being signed out of nowhere.

"It was just being in the right type of band at the right type of time," said Fenix TX's Will Salazar. "Right in that era were pop-punk was getting big…but for whatever reason, being in the right tours, and the right circles."

Growing up on Jawbreaker and the Descendents, The Ataris were one of the prototypical pop-punk bands; DIY-beginnings, songs about love, breakups, traveling the country, and of course, breaking free from the confines of Anytown, USA. Kris Roe and co. went from the small town of Anderson, Indiana to a national notoriety with a gold major label album *So Long, Astoria* that included the cover of Don Henley's "Boys of Summer."

The Ataris spent previous years on small labels like Kung Fu Records—the label headed by Joe Escalante from The Vandals. They were touring in vans, playing the Warped Tour and small clubs along the way; a path pretty much every punk/pop-punk band had to take at one point.

Success doesn't last forever, and not all these bands had storybook endings. The Ataris, after being ran through the major-label ringer, saw the other side of the industry. At one point in The Ataris career, Roe had to resort to selling lyric sheets, and his gold albums, on eBay.

Not all the bands of this era stuck to playing music that would blast through Hot Topic. Panic! At The Disco graduated from the emo scene to one of the biggest pop bands today. Sonny Moore went from fronting **screamo** group From First to Last the world of EDM (electronic dance music) as Skrillex, and became an international DJ star. After Midtown, Gabe Saporta started the dance/pop group Cobra Starship, and now runs a talent management firm. Hayley Williams is now a household name outside of Paramore, and started the hair dye company Good

Dye Young in 2016.

Others made a career out of touring, and some continue touring to this day in order to pay bills. There's still an audience for the All-American Rejects. The Starting Line still gets big East Coast crowds. Brand New was one of the most in-demand bands on the planet. The members of Taking Back Sunday have all done well for themselves. Fall Out Boy live in mansions. My Chemical Romance's success allowed Gerard Way a career in comic books, including a Netflix series adaptation of "The Umbrella Academy". They were able to put My Chemical Romance on "indefinite hiatus" status at the peak of the band's popularity.

"I just started a band because I wanted to play in a hard core scene and have my friends mosh and sing along, and then go to the diner and eat cheese fries. That was it," said The MovieLife's Vinnie Caruana.

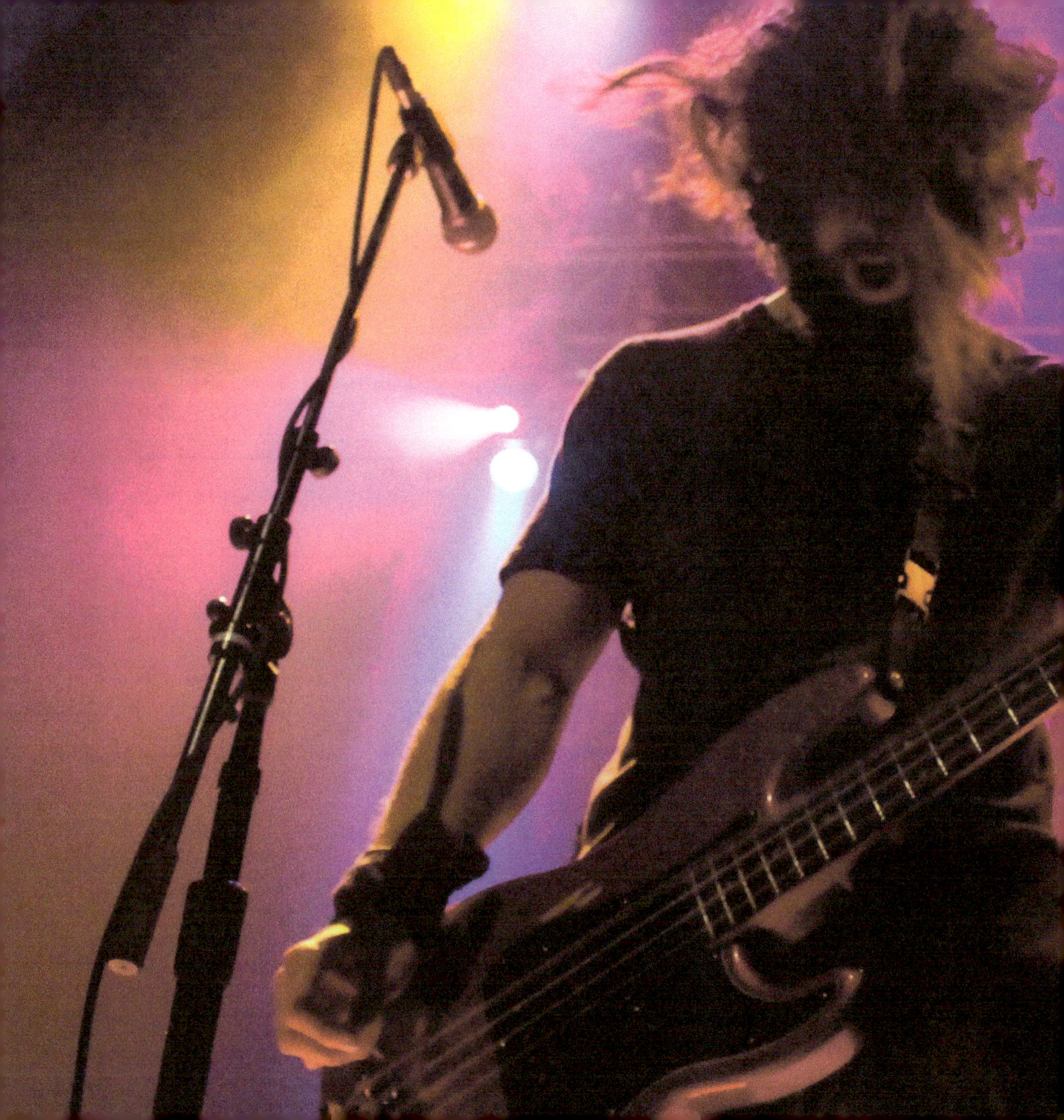

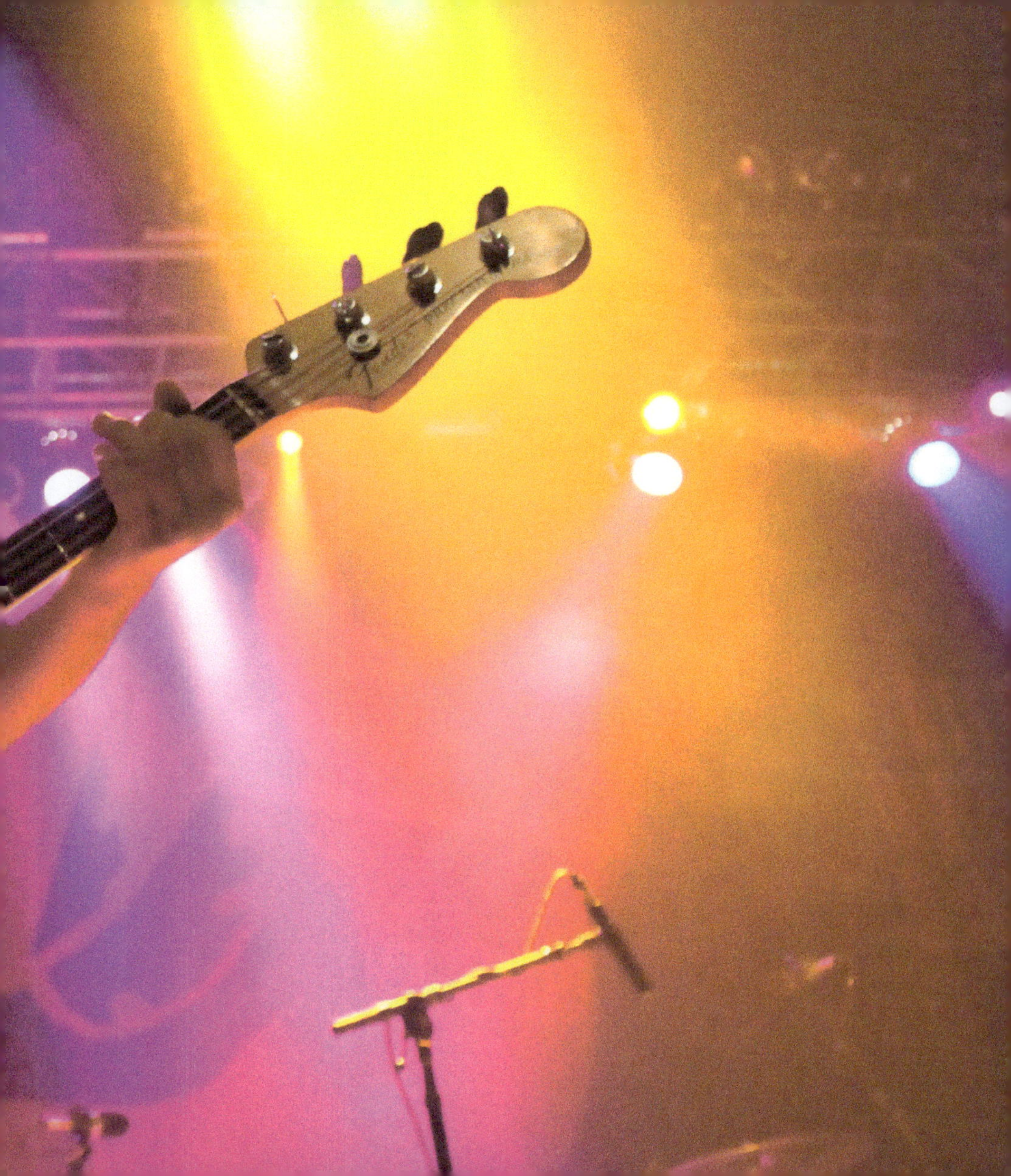

YOU'RE NOT PUNK

AND I'M TELLING EVERYONE

Pop-punk's success has been mostly cyclical. As years progressed, the bands being considered included in the genre sounded less like actual pop-punk and more like pop-rock. The Fueled by Ramen roster led by Fall Out Boy, Panic at the Disco, Paramore, and Gym Class Heroes helped attract a new Warped Tour audience.

Fall Out Boy graduated from being **Absolutepunk.net** favorites to one of the biggest acts in rock music. Their wave introduced acts that were even softer than the bands that came before. All Time Low hit it big by perfecting the line-blurring formula of boy-ish charms with rock songs, all while citing pop-punk as an influence.

Now, the punk-rock police have always been out in full when it comes to pop-punk band's success. Green Day became labeled as sellouts, blink-182 bashing was all the rage in 1999 and purists panned Fall Out Boy.

Green Day came from the same scene of The Queers and Operation Ivy. Blink-182 was influenced by pop-punk legends like Descendents and Screeching Weasel. Fall Out Boy was able to take the poppiest aspects of pop-punk and make it work for pop radio. Fueled By Ramen bands began expanding softer avenues that Fall Out Boy were exploring with Paramore, Panic! At The Disco, Gym Class Heroes, fun., The Academy Is…, and Cobra Starship all on the roster at some point. Fueled By Ramen continues to sign hit-makers to this day.

Again, it's all cyclical, because once a new wave of pop-punk bands washes up on shore, the previous bands that had been bashed by the punk police suddenly weren't that bad after all.

Green Day has been forgiven and now celebrated, the same people who used to bag on blink-182 are now taking their own kids to the band's shows and hey, Fall Out Boy's earlier records are good when putting them side-by-side with the "boy bands with guitars" of the world.

Some good did come out of this latter era, as Paramore's *Riot!* became an instant neo-classic to the scene. The album made them Warped Tour legends and they sky-rocketed to being one of the biggest bands on the planet, with Hayley Williams being crowned the unofficial queen of the scene. Williams released a solo project "Petals For Armor," which was a critically acclaimed indie rock hit in 2020. Fall Out Boy went in more of a pop direction, and are all over the radio and commercials to this day.

The scene was communal, and it was rare for the criticisms of the bands to be truly internal. Generally, the bands didn't attack each other. For the most part, the hate didn't come from the bands themselves, rather fickle fans or kids on message boards. Elder statesman in punk and pop-punk understand the natural progression of sound, and many weren't jealous of the success for other acts they helped pave the way for. On comment sections and message boards on absolutepunk.net or punknews.org, that argument over how punk one band was, or the decisions the band made, were always hotly debated. Even mega-online punk retailer interpunk.com's product review sections became a measuring stick for what was punk and what was not, according to the reviewers.

"When Green Day and blink first came out, I was a big fan from the very beginning," said Milo Aukerman from the Descendents. "I kind of saw it as the next evolution of what we were doing. I will go to my grave listening to pop-punk music, so it is easier for me to embrace what they were doing and not have this territoriality about it. We obviously influenced bands like them, but we were influenced by bands before us, so I feel comfortable being the link in the chain going from the Buzzcocks and the Ramones to Green Day and blink-182."

Photo (p44-45): Shawna Potter of War On Women is also the author of the book: "Making Spaces Safer: A Guide to Giving Harassment the Boot Wherever You Work, Play, and Gather."

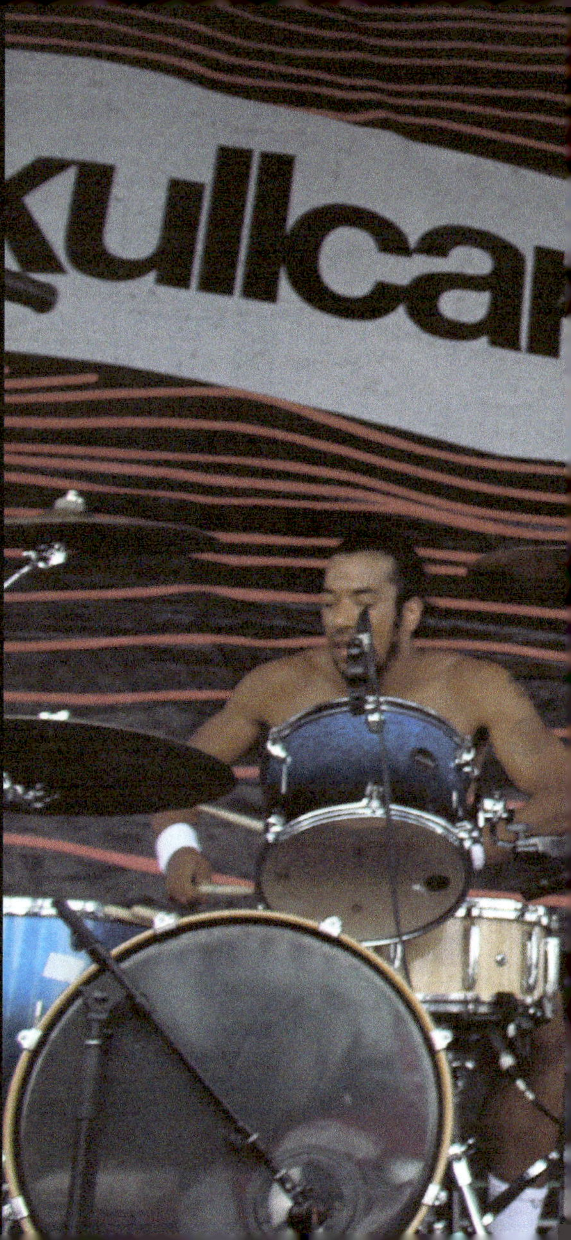

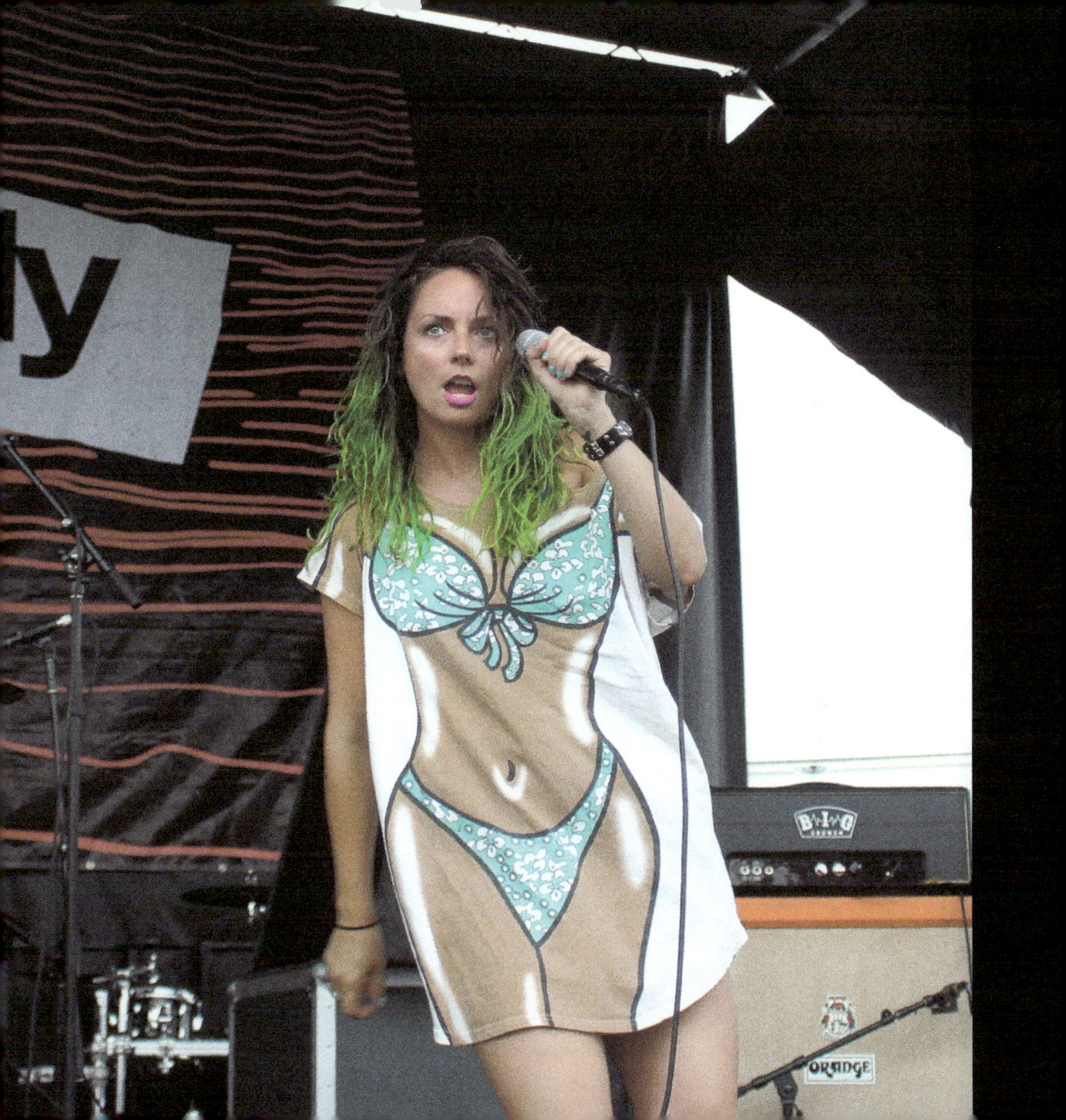
ORANGE

I WANT TO BE STEREOTYPED

I WANT TO BE CLASSIFIED

Skateboarding and punk culture always went hand-in-hand, with the Epitaph and Fat Wreck Chords bands defining the sound as the songs from Epitaph's "Punk-o'Rama" compilations were soon featured on Tony Hawk video games. The X-Games would go on to feature acts like blink-182, All Time Low, Wavves and Bad Religion performing at the action sports Olympics.

What started as a hobby of skateboarding and playing songs of love gone wrong became career opportunities for many. It was an inevitable marriage of misfits that started in the 1980s as skateboarding and punk culture merged. The rebellious nature of the music, and the fast and furious sounds of the songs were a perfect match for the live fast, die young lifestyle of skating. It wasn't just the streets of Southern California; skateboarding was a global phenomenon. The influence spread all over the world, which was a testament to music's power overall. Skate culture merging with punk occured globally as evident by international bands like Millencolin and Refused. Skating, surfing, BMX and other action sports started to become recognized as official sports, and punk music was the official soundtrack to it.

"For me, that whole era, we were always playing punk rock," said avid skateboarder Matt Skiba of Alkaline Trio, blink-182, Heavens,and Matt Skiba and the Sekrets. "Sort of like skating…you start doing something because you love, and then you start doing it for a job, it's a dream come true. As cliché as that sounds it is what it is."

On an episode of The Simpsons titled "Barting Over," Bart finds out he used to be a child star, but Homer Simpson blew all of the money he made. A defiant Bart then runs away, and eventually ends up at a loft party hosted by skate boarding's Tony Hawk, and blink-182 was the musical guest.

With pop-punk becoming cool, the skater culture and lifestyle soon started taking over shopping malls. Girls started to date skater boys who were edgy, but not quite alarming enough to worry mom and dad that much. Hot Topic became a bastardized poster child for commercial punk consumerism.

Kids were hitting up PacSun for all the cool skate brands their favorite artists would wear like Hurley, Volcom and Vans. Skate and surf culture clothing lines, like Hurley, would sponsor bands;unfortunately, this would lead to more arguments about the commercialization of punk.

 Musicians started to buy in too, as bands would form lifestyle lines of their own with Travis Barker's Famous Stars and Straps, Simple Plan's Role Model, the Mark-Hoppus and Tom DeLonge ventures in Atticus and Macbeth Footwear, and Good Charlotte's MADE all taking off. The musicians were now getting corporate sponsorship, and free swag from clothing companies, skate companies and action/lifestyle brands. Your favorite rock stars were now dabbling on the side as businessmen with stakes in their own clothing companies. This idea of entrepreneurship was prevalent in hip-hop, but now pop-punk bands were smartening up, and cashing in.

The Atticus clothing line started up in 2001, founded by Tom DeLonge, Mark Hoppus, and their childhood friend Dylan Anderson. "The idea behind Atticus was to be a music brand [fashion line] so that kids didn't have to wear a surf or skate tee anymore when they didn't even play those sports; that you would see someone with an Atticus tee and know instantly that they were into the same music that you were," said Anderson, current brand manager for Hi My Name Is Mark. "The year 2001 was the kick off for Atticus, and for the emo scene pretty much. The fashion at the time was very preppy and pastel, which didn't go well with the emerging black-on-black-on black punk/emo look."

Jocks and cheerleaders started going to these types of emo and pop-punk shows. Your favorite bands were showing up in magazines marketed for teen girls. Pop-punk and emo went from the underground to the forefront of popular culture. This was just a mere symptom of when something that starts out small become big, and the inevitable elitism and backlash followed. Your favorite band went from playing coffee shops to arenas, and you were there from the beginning, which gave you a sense of superiority over the "poseurs" who just got into them because they were on MTV. At times the cultural clash was with newer fans who were unaware of the ethos behind the music, and were there just simply for the music.

So, what did fans of this era look like?

Pop-punk dress code check list:

-Chuck Taylors or Vans

- Dickies shorts

-Socks that went above your ankles

-Bracelet or band logo sweat band on wrist

-Studded belt (belt buckle optional, but the Famous Stars and Straps iconic "F" badge was always a good choice.)

-Band T-shirt

-Sideways or backwards baseball hat. Fitted New Era hats of Major League Baseball team became a thing here too, as a way for fans to ironically rep the same towns they were trying to escape.

This style eventually became just as clichéd as eating pizza, or tattoos and piercings, and to "leave this town" archetypes found in the songs.

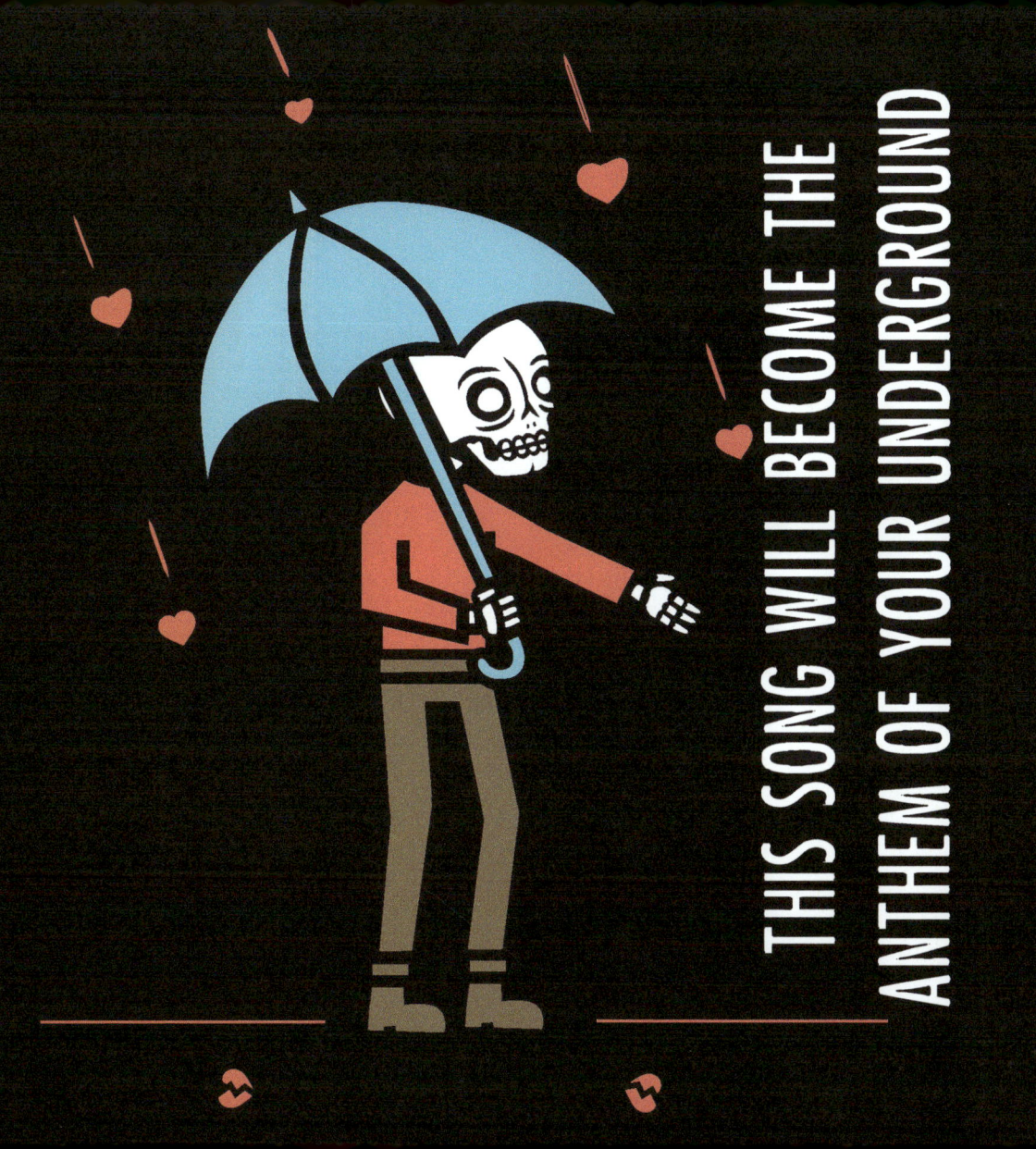

THIS SONG WILL BECOME THE ANTHEM OF YOUR UNDERGROUND

There was an immediate connection to pop-punk as the songs became underdog anthems to the freaks, the nerds and the romantics. The songs were easily relatable. The emo movement especially pulled in kids who felt like they didn't belong anywhere else, but now had a place, just like the punk rock scene did ages ago. It drew in the pop-punk kids who weren't quite accepted by the Dead Kennedys and Anti-Flag crowds, but got by on MxPx and Sum 41.

The movement's meaning was obvious when you listened to Chris Carrabba command a crowd of kids, each of them singing along to every word. Even the non-punk/pop-punk crowd could relate because the songs, and themes the bands were writing about were universal. The rest of the world got a glimpse of this when Carrabba performed an *MTV Unplugged* episode. For those watching, Dashboards Confessional's influence over all those kids would have them believe the emo fans were cult-like in their support.

Everyone has been screwed over and lied to by an ex, passed over for someone else, and felt like an outsider. Teenage angst went beyond being shackled by parental and societal rules. Kids found a voice in these songs and an outlet. To many, these weren't just songs; they were anthems written by underdogs, just like the very listeners consuming the music. People who were just like them, grew up like them or experienced similar hardships and heartbreaks, were speaking to them through distorted guitars and whiny vocals.

But now, they didn't have to feel alone. The music, and scene, bred a sense of community that spilled over to an already growing innovation in societal interactions: the Internet and the birth of social media. The boom of Myspace allowed users to interact with each other, follow artists/celebrities and business accounts, post photos and thoughts, and fostered one of the first platforms for this newfound interaction model. The cultural impact aside, these sites were content and money generators. News Corp paid $580 million to acquire the rights to Myspace in 2005. By 2007, Myspace was valued at over $12 billion; websites started popping up that took advantage of the community model through message boards, registered users, and plenty of other opportunities for music fans to interact with each other.

Once a fan site for MxPx and blink-182, Absolutepunk.net grew into something that assisted in popularizing bands to the next level of stardom. In 2000, Jason Tate founded Absolutepunk.net, which was an alt-music news website, and online community. At one point in the site's heyday, they had over 300,000 registered users. In 2005, the site hit its peak traffic with six million hits daily, which put high-profile sites like Myspace on notice. Blender even named Tate No. 18 in their "Top 25 Most Influential People in Online Music" article.

In print, **Alternative Press** was a long-running alt music magazine that, in its early days, offered cutting-edge coverage of up-and-coming artists. The coverage shifted heavier to the Warped Tour crowd in the early 2000s, which led to increased ad space, and overall page count. The monthly print publication grew during this time, and eventually was able to branch out to do its own red carpet awards ceremonies.

"Working at Alternative Press during emo's explosion into the mainstream was equal parts thrilling and confusing," said former staff writer and editor Scott Heisel. "For a stretch in the mid-2000s, every single issue we put out became our biggest issue ever. So many bands were selling so many records, which in turn sent more advertising dollars our way, which in turn meant the editorial and art staff at AP would work countless extra hours to crank out a finished product we were proud of, and that did its best to comprehensively cover what we lovingly dubbed 'Warped Tour Nation.'"

Open forum sites' biggest effect was giving the youth an outlet online to comfortably discuss bands, sports, even politics and other issues. If kids couldn't talk about these subjects in school, or had social anxiety, online forums gave them a voice. The bands and label took notice too, and used sites like Absolutepunk.net and the forum comments to gauge their audience and see what was working, and what was not. These early days of social media really set the blueprint for what we now have in 2020 with Twitter, Instagram, Facebook, TikTok, and other forms of social media.

The underdog/outsider mentality still existed even with this music growing in popularity. Fans were able to find common allies in the bands that looked like them, acted like them, and grew up like them. Emo and pop-punk kids were misfits just like the punk rockers, goths and metal heads, but safer.

"All three of us were born and raised in Southern California," said blink-182's Mark Hoppus. "We grew up in this culture. We were all the ones in high school that were being made fun of because we were skaters and punk rockers and heavy metalers and losers, and it's just a part of our identity."

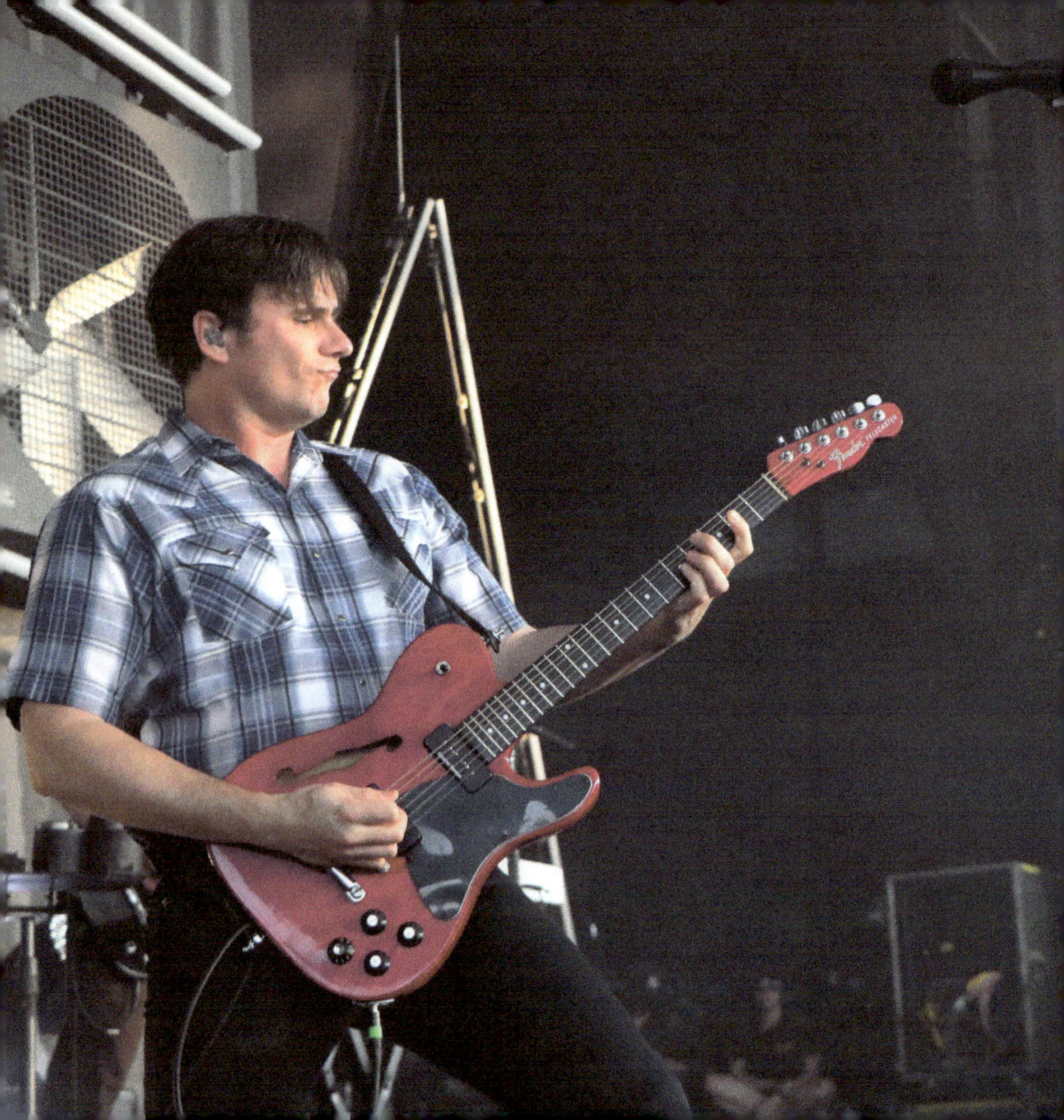

I GUESS THIS IS GROWING UP

Many of the bands that ruled the scene are a lot older now, but luckily, longevity has followed some acts. There is camaraderie among the groups still standing by outliving the trends and staying true. Bands like Bayside, All-American Rejects and Saves the Day still have a secure place the modern day touring world.

"All the bands that came up during that time, and are still doing it, we feel really connected," said Saves The Day's Chris Conley. "We all weathered the storm, and are still here rocking out." (No "Shoulder To The Wheel" pun intended).

Too many bands nowadays are in for the wrong reasons, evident by some of the musician's immature, embarrassing behavior and monetary tunnel vision. What sets the bands from this era apart to their modern counterparts is coming from a scene that was built on punk ethos and work ethic.

"We grew up in the suburbs of Fort Lauderdale and we didn't do the band to get famous or have success as a band," said New Found Glory's Chad Gilbert. "We needed something to do and loved music, and to be honest, that is one of reasons I think we are still a band today. We have the same attitude if we are playing a festival in front of 20,000 people or some random city in front of 100 kids."

The dreams that began in bedrooms, with the cliché yet genuine hopes to sell out garages and local bars, and eventually turned into financially viable and rewarding vocations.

"Our initial goal, I remember Dan [Andriano] and I were at Superchunk show in Chicago, and we both got in with fake IDs and were talking about how it would be great to get a following like Superchunk like where every town you play in, you'd get 500 kids," said Alkaline Trio's Matt Skiba. "So, we've exceeded that, and are still pleasantly shocked how well our band does."

All these bands have families now and kids of their own; go watch "The Other F Word," a fantastic documentary on punk rock and fatherhood. They've all aged. Facial hair is more apparent. Dyed hair is replaced by natural greys. The fans feel old too; the folks at a Get Up Kids Show aren't kids anymore. At one memorable Matt Pryor (The Get Up Kids, The New Amsterdams) solo show in Houston, Pryor was opening for Max Bemis of Say Anything fame, and the younger fans were mostly there for Bemis. When Pryor played some older The Get Up Kids songs acoustic, it caused some of the older fans in audience to lightly mosh, which prompted Pryor to momentarily stop the song to jokingly tell the crowd "they were being too punk rock and scaring the kids."

"Having kids changes your outlook on everything," said Pryor, who took his daughter, Lily, on tour to open for his solo shows. "It is the thing where people say 'Having kids changes everything,' and you go, 'Sure, whatever,' and then it happens and you are like F-yeah it really does. I'm a homemaker, stay-at-home dad. I cook, clean, change diapers, chill out, hang out with kids. Normal people stuff."

Not all the bands or musicians continued to play music. Some had to transition from the stage to parenthood, or the job market. For some the transition is smooth, but for others they eventually return to the stage.

"I spent a number of years of heavy touring with a handful of bands," said Tripp Wiggins from Schatzi. "When my oldest son was born, I made the decision to get off the road and focus on being a parent. It was a difficult adjustment to say the least. I was pretty deep in the scene, and had to watch my friends from the sidelines grow their careers, while I changed mine. After a couple of years of turning down gigs, the calls stopped coming. That was the gut punch. The drive I had that pushed me forward in my music career, translated well into a business career though. I did corporate sales and management and then moved on to running my own businesses over the past ten years. I have a few friends that are very successful in the industry and others that never quite made it, but that is all that they know. So, now they are pushing fifty and struggling to make ends meet. I still do some studio recording and I'm playing weekly, but I do it for me...not to pay the bills. I have amazing memories from my time playing and touring, and if I had the opportunity to do it all over again, I wouldn't change a thing."

Since the 1990s, the band's music has matured too. Taking Back Sunday has become more of a true rock band. Blink-182 showed how a progressive pop-punk record should be done on the untitled album, and *Neighborhoods*. Green Day's *American Idiot* spawned a Broadway musical. My Chemical Romance also showed a flair for the theatrical. These are grown men now in their forties and up, so the days of singing about high school, and/or girls are long gone, as they should be.

Longevity and creativity are key elements of the bands' ability to survive and thrive after all these years. When bands age and their tastes mature and change, so does this music. This is something that should be expected, but it isn't always the case from the fan's perspective, as many want bands to stick with the same style, and try to re-create some of their former glory.

"What has allowed blink to last so long is that

we've always written music from the heart, and never thought of ourselves in any specific category or genre," blink-182's Mark Hoppus said. "A lot of bands try to continue to fit into whatever they think that people want them to be and are afraid to grow, and try different things. With blink, we just started off wanting to play fast and loud. … And when Travis (Barker) joined the band, he brought a whole new creative side to it. I don't think there is anything that any of us would write that we would say, 'Oh, that's not blink', because if it comes from our brains, then it's blink."

Bands broke up and reunited. My Chemical Romance, blink-182, The Get Up Kids, Motion City Soundtrack, and others either called it quits or went on indefinite hiatus, occasionally getting back together for lucrative reunion shows and sold-out tours.

"I think that a lot of bands right now have a huge nostalgia following and that reminds us of our youth, so we go out," said Andrew Youngblood, a show promoter with Youngblood Booking. "I know if anything comes through and tours that was from my childhood, I try to go see it because it's probably the last chance I'm going to get."

Senses Fail eloquently captured the essence of still playing in an emo band during 2018 with *If There's A Light It Will Find You*. The lyrics on "Is It

Going To Be The Year" has front man Buddy Nielsen's introspective view:

I've just been screaming to a microphone away from home
When everyone I know gave up a long time ago
What else am I supposed to do with my life?
All that I've ever known are late night drives from Salt Lake City to Seattle to San Fran
I hope I die in the back of a (expletive) van

The sentiment continues on "Double Cross":

While you're watching from the window waiting
I've been spilling my guts out on the stage
I spent the best years of my life drinking myself to sleep at night
And now the glory days have all, but faded
Everyone I used to know is jaded
Where is the passion that you used to have?
When music was the only thing that you had?

SAVE YOUR GENERATION

The Warped Tour, which has been a scene staple for over 20 years, is more than just punk rock summer camp. The traveling festival had become one of the longest running summer tours and has helped launch the careers of musical heavyweights Eminem, No Doubt, Katy Perry, Gym Class Heroes, and, of course, has hosted the punk and pop-punk scenes stars since its inception. In 2018, the tour completed its final proper North American run. In 2019, tour founder Kevin Lyman booked three Warped Tour festival dates in Ohio, California and New Jersey to celebrate the end of the tour's legacy. Those last three dates were some of tour's largest in size, paid attendance, and lineup depth.

For many kids, the Warped Tour was a badge of honor, or initiation into punk, skate and **scene** culture. First, you'd have to weather harsh summer temperatures, as well as the sensory overload of merchandise tents, multiple stages, and frantically trying to locate the set times of the day. The grueling heat was also a challenge for the bands and crew, who were up and working well before the gates opened at 11 a.m.

"I think with Warped Tour, you have to have a little bit of everything because there's groups of people who like different kinds of music," said New Found Glory's Ian Grushka. "And that makes it special; people coming together whether you like heavier music or ska or punk rock—that is what made Warped Tour cool when I was growing up."

Every night the order and set times would change, which meant on each date, the show would have a different band closing. So, while some bands ranked higher on the placement of tour posters due to popularity, relevance and stardom, each night there would be a different **headliner**, which helped try to eliminate ego and rock star mentality. Even with varying set changes, the tour ran like a well-oiled machine due to the work of Lyman, Lisa Brownlee, and their team behind the scenes. While the tour had the structures in place to fully function, every day still felt different due to the unpredictability of crowds, weather, and other factors.

"Any time I prepare for a tour like this, everything I prepared for doesn't happen," said Andy Williams from Every Time I Die. "You kind of don't know what to expect."

The tour also offered accessibility with bands hanging out at the merch tent, musician workshops, and informative tents that fit with the under-dog causes like PETA, Action For Animals, truth.com and others.

The Vans sponsorship of Warped Tour began in 1996. The leader in skateboarding shoes and culture made for an obvious choice to sponsor a traveling rock festival with ramps, skate demos, skate-punk bands, and punk activism.

"I don't think Warped Tour ever really left its roots

as maybe the tastes changed and new genres were born," said Kevin Bivona from ska-punk act the Interrupters. "The fact that Warped Tour has been going for this many years is a testimonial to the fact they do stay current."

Trying to foster a family environment, "punk rock summer camp" as it was aptly nicknamed, the tour also served as a reunion of sorts for the bands, crews, and tour organizers. Besides getting the chance to play and entice new fans, bands like Motion City Soundtrack also used the tour as an opportunity to catch up with old friends and promote a good cause.

"We've been friends with The All-American Rejects for a long time, so it is always fun to see them play and hang out," Motion City Soundtrack bassist Matt Taylor said.

Motion City Soundtrack also helped fund a new venture called "Give A Little Help", aimed to provide an outlet for youth and to provide rewards to charities.

"We get a lot of e-mails and people who come through with meet-and-greets and signings and they are like, 'I don't need you to sign anything; I just want to say your music means a lot to me,'" said Taylor. "We wanted to do something where people can have an outlet when they need some sort of help."

While the tour has had its fair share of criticism, mostly about the commercialization of punk and associated sponsorships, and in later years the inclusion of certain bands and people, the tour has become a go-to event for the entire scene. It has grown tremendously from simply being an alternative rock/punk tour.

The diversified lineup always gives bands old and new the chance to connect to new crowds. Bands with established followings like Yellowcard, who hit it big in the 2000s, may be a new discover for the tour's younger fan base.

"We are always excited for the opportunity to make new fans, and that's a good thing about the Warped Tour; no matter how big or small your band is, there is a chance for someone who has never heard your music before to hear it," said Yellowcard's Ryan Key. "We are grateful for Warped Tour to give us the opportunity to continue to make new fans."

As bands like Less Than Jake, Reel Big Fish, and Rancid get older, it's harder for them to commit to the grueling summer trek. And with trends ever-changing, the Taking Back Sundays and New Found Glorys of the world have become the "veteran" bands on the bill. The tour has recently scaled back booking emo and traditional pop-punk bands, adding EDM (electronic dance music), more metal, and more pop to the lineup, but new scene bands like The Wonder Years are still included as well."

"The music has definitely changed, but I feel,

like, the attitude and punk rock-ness of putting all these different styles of music together; via country to electronic to screaming, crazy hardcore to pop-punk," said Simple Plan's Pierre Bouvier. "It's kind of cool how this all fits under one umbrella."

While there is much to adore about Vans Warped Tour, it hasn't always been flawless. The tour was faced with criticism by booking Front Porch Step, an alleged sex offender at the time, and a petition was signed by over 13,000 people to prevent him from playing the dates he was booked. It was assumed he dropped off the tour, but when he showed up to Nashville stop to play the acoustic tent, he was faced with protest from fans and other artists on the bill.

Warped Tour tried to save face by booking more female-fronted acts like the Interrupters and the feminist punk band War On Women in coming years.

"It's vital for people to support Warped Tour when they are making these efforts to be more inclusive," said Shawna Potter from War On Women. "It is important we are here to offer an alternative to some of the other bands that really don't care about women at all. I want to be that alternative and that other voice."

A Voice For The Innocent (AVFTI) is a non-profit organization that helps victims of sexual abuse. AVFTI got to spread its message on the Warped Tour as one of the many activism booths allowed on tour to help spread the message and create safe spaces for attendees.

"As a two-time Warped attendee and two-time survivor of sexual assault, the issues the tour faces are glaringly obvious to me," said promotional director of AVFTI Kristen Eby. "Unfortunately, music festivals of this size—especially ones with such a young fanbase—provide ample opportunity for sexual assault and abuse of power, as evidenced by the numerous allegations against musicians over the years and stories of fan-on-fan harassment. A Voice For The Innocent is part of a massive push to fight that the culture that breeds this behavior and support anyone who's been negatively affected. We give people a place to go, and a way to have their voices heard. My experience has been overwhelmingly positive. Musicians are supportive and fans are appreciative. As does everyone on the tour, we work long hours in tough conditions—but being face-to-face with survivors who trust us and are grateful for our presence makes it totally worth it."

The tour also has had other booths on awareness like the suicide prevention organization To Write Love On Her Arms (TWLOHA), which has been involved in this scene for years. With the recent suicide-related deaths to Linkin Park's Chester Bennington and Audioslave's Chris Cornell, the rock world needs groups like this more than ever. With impressionable youth worshipping these bands and artists, it is important for the kids at home to know that help exists.

"You never know what a kid can be carrying or struggling with when they walk through these gates," said Elizabeth Wilder, music and event coordinator for TWLOHA. "Music is a safe place; we want to be that bridge between the music and the help you can get just by walking up to our tent. With the passing of so many singers, we want to be here to say 'you are not alone and it is okay to not be okay' and we are here for you."

Warped Tour slightly rebounded from its image problem, and avoided the potential public relations nightmare.

The tour has become a rite of passage for bands. Bands that play it a badge of honor knowing they survived the heat and the grind.

"It's gnarly awful to eat out of Styrofoam plates for eight weeks and be in parking lots," said blink-182's Tom DeLonge. "But the tour is amazing, and it's this cultural circus that has become a national pastime at this point. It's one of the most necessary, and raddest tours out there. It's just really hard to do for eight weeks."

Even with supportive genres, tensions can rise with so many personalities crammed together for such a long tour. There was the inevitable culture clash with older bands like NOFX, Dickies, and Guttermouth conflicting with the newer kids and their core beliefs. Fat Mike from NOFX made it a habit to poke fun at the Underoaths of the world, and other Christian bands on tour. "Underoath doesn't believe in dinosaurs"(an age-old creationism versus evolution jab) was a common joke hurled from one stage to another. Fat Mike's ribbing of the Warped Tour mates was caught on camera by music television network Fuse, which was documenting the Warped Tour for a TV special. In one portion, vocal atheist Fat Mike sat in on a Bible study at Warped Tour, which intrinsically sounds like an odd thing, but also showed the generational divide between the younger bands and veteran artists on the tour. The Fuse episode showed how after the Bible study session, Fat Mike was approached by Dango from Amber Pacific, who was a part of the Bible reading. Dango professed his love for NOFX to Fat Mike, and told him his band and album *Punk In Public* were the reasons he started playing this style of music. This specific scene on the Fuse special showed that even though there was an age gap, and cultural differences on the tour, there were still common bonds to unite the Vans Warped Tour: namely music.

Ultimately, the tour served generations of concert goers an experience that transcended the tour's skate punk early beginnings. Fans were able to discover acts like Eminem, Katy Perry, Paramore, Fall Out Boy and countless others that would cross over to superstardom. Older punk bands were able to bridge the generational divides between the past, and future, and later tours would try to mimic the formula.

There have been simlar tours like Rockstar Energy's Taste Of Chaos tour, which was also the brain-child of Lyman, that had moderate success. Rockstar Energy tried to keep it up with 2019's Disrupt tour with Circa Survive, Thrice, The Used, Atreyu and others, but had low-ticket sales. No other tour really captured the spirit and success that the Vans Warped Tour did, despite many attempts.

THE PAST IS ONLY THE FUTURE WITH THE LIGHTS ON

The resurgence of the emo and pop-punk scene has paid dividends for older acts who helped set the bar for punk rock. Riot Fest, which features the cream of the crop for all eras of the genre, made waves by reuniting the original Misfits for the festival one year, and bringing Jawbreaker out of retirement the next.

The inverse of preserving the past is keeping up with the changing times. Releasing new music, utilizingmodern branding (such as beer and coffee), adding to the legacy and developing a new era—allof this is part of Milo Aukerman' and the Descendents' new lease on life.

Time has always worked in favor of the Descendents, and for Aukerman, the chips fell perfectly in place for the band to go semi-full force again. For over thirty years on-and-off, the Descendents have been the Godfathers of pop-punk, bridging the gap between the Buzzcocks to blink-182, and touching every band in between. The band picked up steam again after the fantastic documentary "Filmage" and countless successful festival appearances.

"It's been a big challenge to finally consider music a career," said Aukerman, who left his job as a research biologist at DuPont to return to the Descendents full-time. "Once you start viewing music as a career, it's something you no longer do just for fun."

The pop-punk/emo heyday skyrocketed bands,

and changed lives of not only the artists involved, but also the millions of listeners they influenced. All of the bands tapped into an energy of youth yearning for an expression of their angst and heartbreaks. It was a time when bubble gum pop reigned supreme for too long, radio rock was bland, and George W Bush and his administration were in control. Kids wanted an outlet for rebellion; a raised fist that wasn't too threatening, but necessary.

"That's really when our bands coalesced," said blink-182's Mark Hoppus. "That's when we found our legs, found our sound, and I have great memories from that time."

To see the popularity of the emo revival, look no further than the monthly emo nights popping up around clubs and bars all around the country. "Taking Back Tuesday," aka Emo Night LA, is one of the biggest examples. Once a month, clubs and bars are devoted to emo punk, and for Los Angeles, includes band performances from the likes of Dashboard Confessional, and celebrity guest DJs such as Mikey Way of MCR, and Hoppus of blink-182. These events often look like concerts, with mosh pits and shout-alongs overtaking the dance floors, and beloved music videos on the screens. There's popular emo nights in Brooklyn, San Francisco (Diary), Boston, Philadelphia (Through Being Cool), Cleveland (cleverly titled Jukebox Breakdown), Austin (Jimmy Eat Wednesday), Houston (Saves The Tuesday) and many other major U.S. cities.

Taking Back Tuesday wasn't the first emo night, but the Los Angeles version garnered the most steam. Barbara Szabo, T.J. Petracca and Morgan Freed had simply wanted to throw themed parties, but soon emo night turned into a national craze. It became big enough that the three friends behind Taking Back Tuesday even filed to trademark the phrase "Emo Night."

Houston Emo Club founder Alex Chavez spearheaded bringing these events to East Texas after getting fired from Barbarella, a well known club, for playing Britney Spears at a 1980s-themed night. He came back to the bar with an idea of doing an emo/pop-punk night, and the rest is history. Chavez's goal was to make "Saves The Tuesday" and "Jimmy Eat Wednesday" feel like a community-led scene by incorporating locals as guest DJs.

"The emo club, in my mind, is everyone that goes and people who still love all this stuff," said Chavez. "The only reason the night is a ton of fun is because of everyone involved."

These emo-themed nights helped prove that there was a keen interest in scene that had never really died, just had to be revived to the masses. It isn't just people in their thirties at these things; kids of all ages have come out to sing and dance along to the songs of an era that isn't that far behind. Frequently the bars and clubs are at maximum capacity, with fans line up outside well before open, just like they would for an actual show. Sometimes, the kids at these events are literal kids.

"The emo nights in general are incredible; the one in L.A. especially gets special consideration for being the first one to go out there and defy the sentiment of the day, which was at the time: the [emo/punk] music was corny to like...and it has turned into something massive," said Chris Carrabba of Dashboard Confessional. "Just like our scene was built in the first place, this seems to be built on the fans that like it and [who] will take it upon themselves to make it popular."

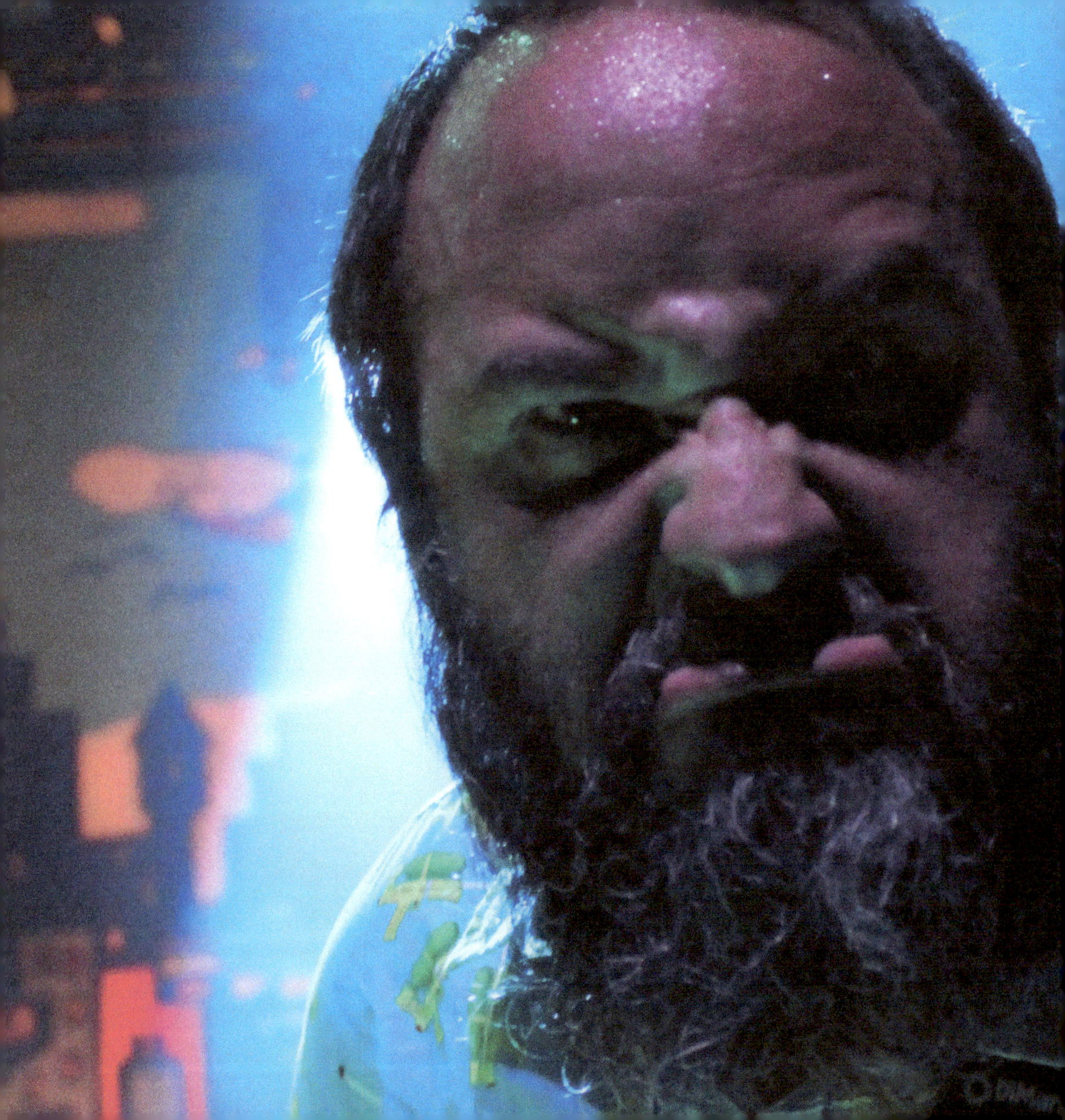

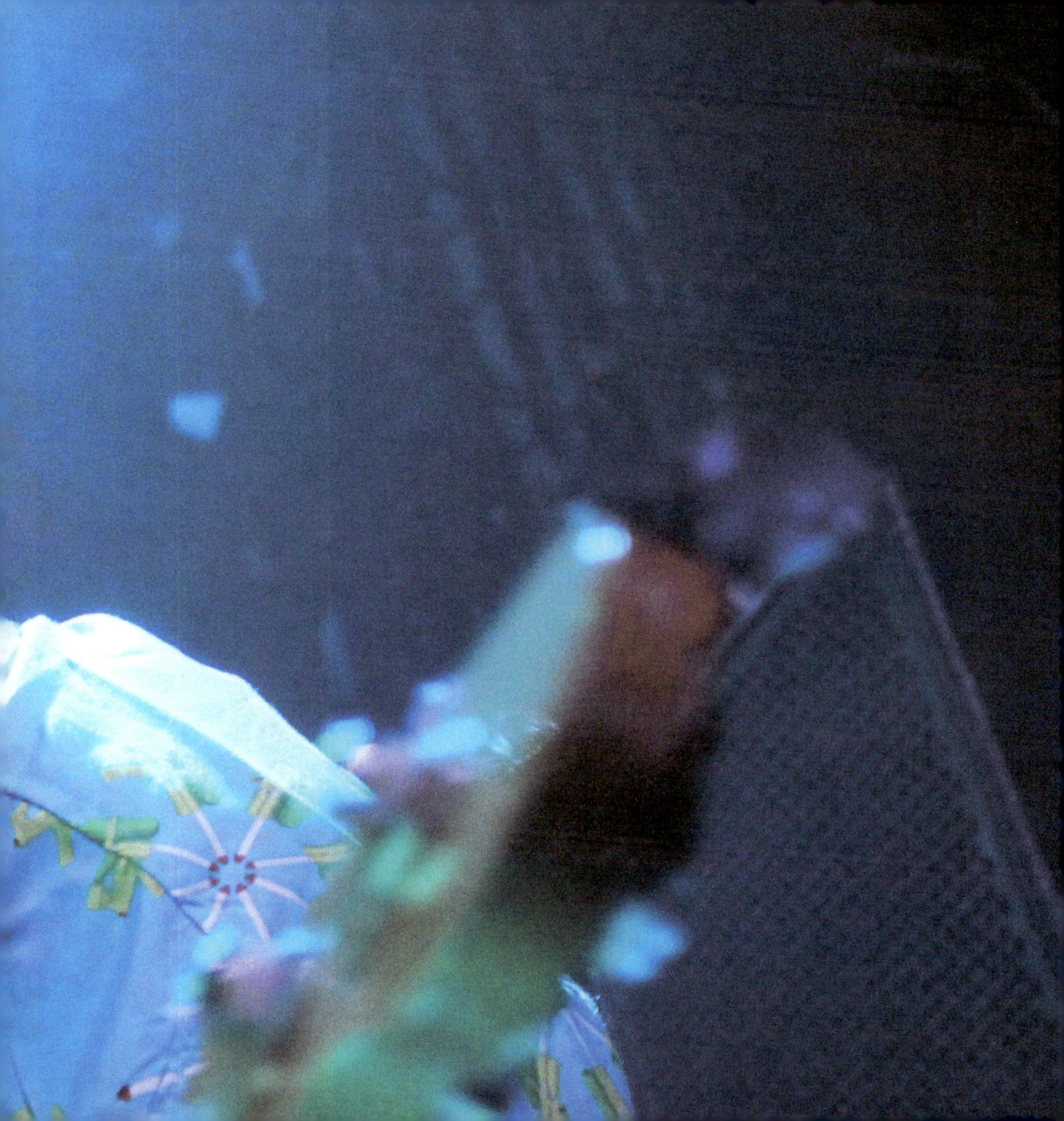

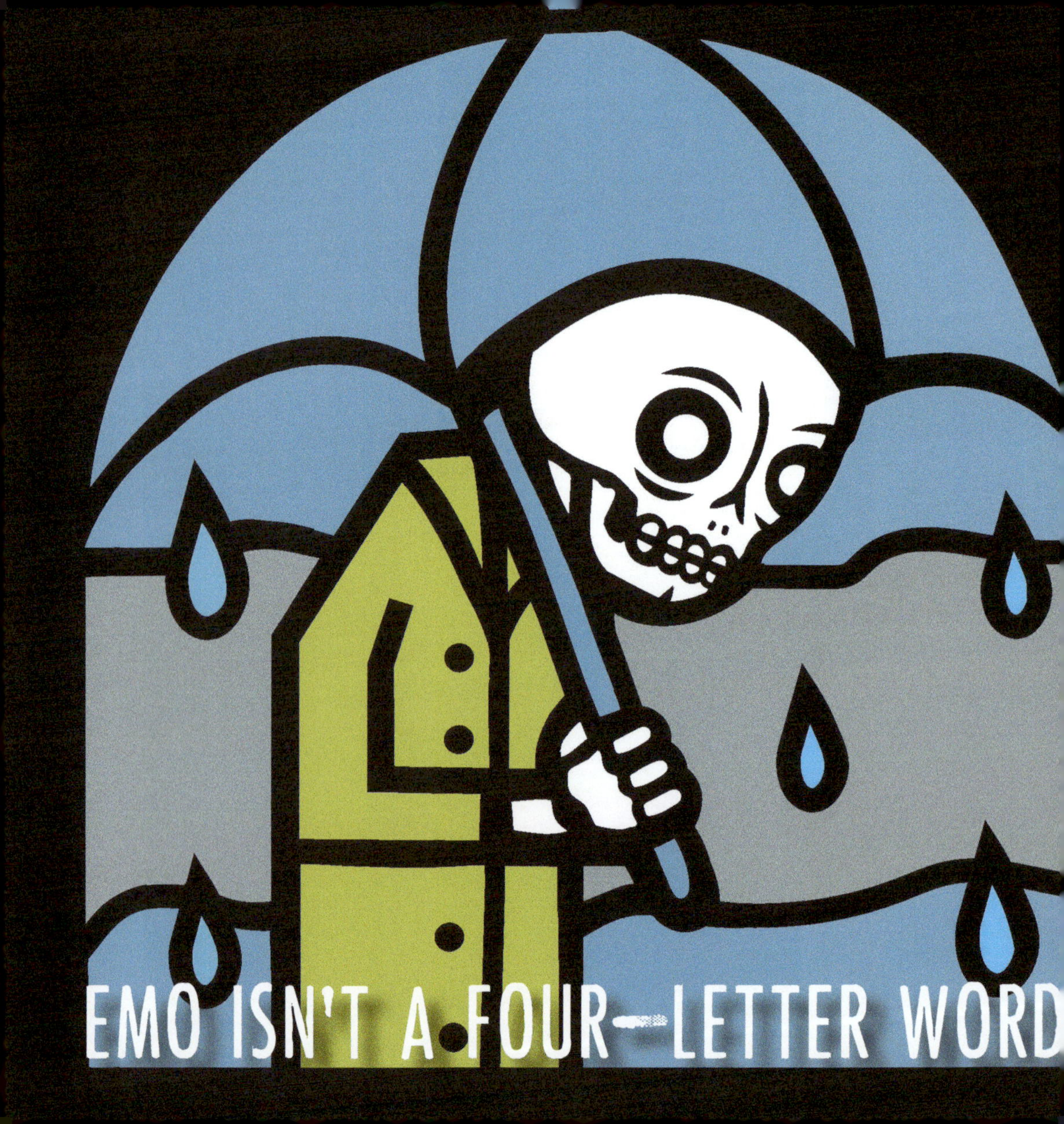
EMO ISN'T A FOUR-LETTER WORD

There was a time when the term emo elicited shudders in response, as a sea of clones with emo-swoop hair, eyeliner, and black nail polish saturated the scene. Sunny Day Real Estate, Mineral, Texas Is The Reason, and acts like Rites Of Spring were soon deemed with the emo tag. Now it hangs on Hawthorne Heights and Say Anything.

While the 1990s rock scene was ripe with grunge, alternative, as well as punk-rock's coming out party, many of the independent bands of that era were making underground waves. Even the music that came from the mainstream during that era felt more emotional and connected than the hair metal that reigned supreme before it.

"We are not an emo band, but we've been called 'architects of emo,'" said Stephan Jenkins of the mega alt-rock act Third Eye Blind. "Some article was sent to me years ago about me and Billy Corgan [Smashing Pumpkins] being architects of emo, and I was like what the (expletive) is emo?"

While bands like Braid and The Promise Ring did get new-found attention during the era, emo soon became co-opted by the Hot Topic crowd, sparking debates on the difference between emo and goth kids. The term emo became a poster child for a certain fashion sense and a way to describe the outsider kids.

"They were calling us emo for a long time because

we have personal songs; one of our biggest influences is Jawbreaker," said Alkaline Trio's Matt Skiba. "No matter what category anyone puts us in, personal-emotive music is kind of cathartic. I'm glad to feel like we kind of stand separate from everything. The Descendents...all those bands influenced all of us, so it is pop-punk rock music, so I don't take any offense to that at all."

The emo craze also helped catapult the likes of Dashboard Confessional, Jimmy Eat World, and My Chemical Romance.

"It was incredibly important, it was important to me," said Chris Carrabba. "We were almost polar opposites to the style of music that was popular at the time, and if anything is popular long enough it will be knocked down a peg, so maybe it wasn't the worst thing in the world for us to be knocked down a little while."

While emo never died, the trend aspect of it did die down, even though the fans of the bands remained loyal after the peak in popularity. To this day acts like AFI, Thrice, Taking Back Sunday, The Used and Dashboard Confessional still sell out large clubs and venues around the world.

"We went away for a bit ourselves, so we sort of side stepped the backlash, but not by design and certainly we were not unaware of it," said Carrabba. "We really had to pinch ourselves; traveling all around and playing in front of these audiences, and still to this day, the people are still there with us, and it's pretty glorious."

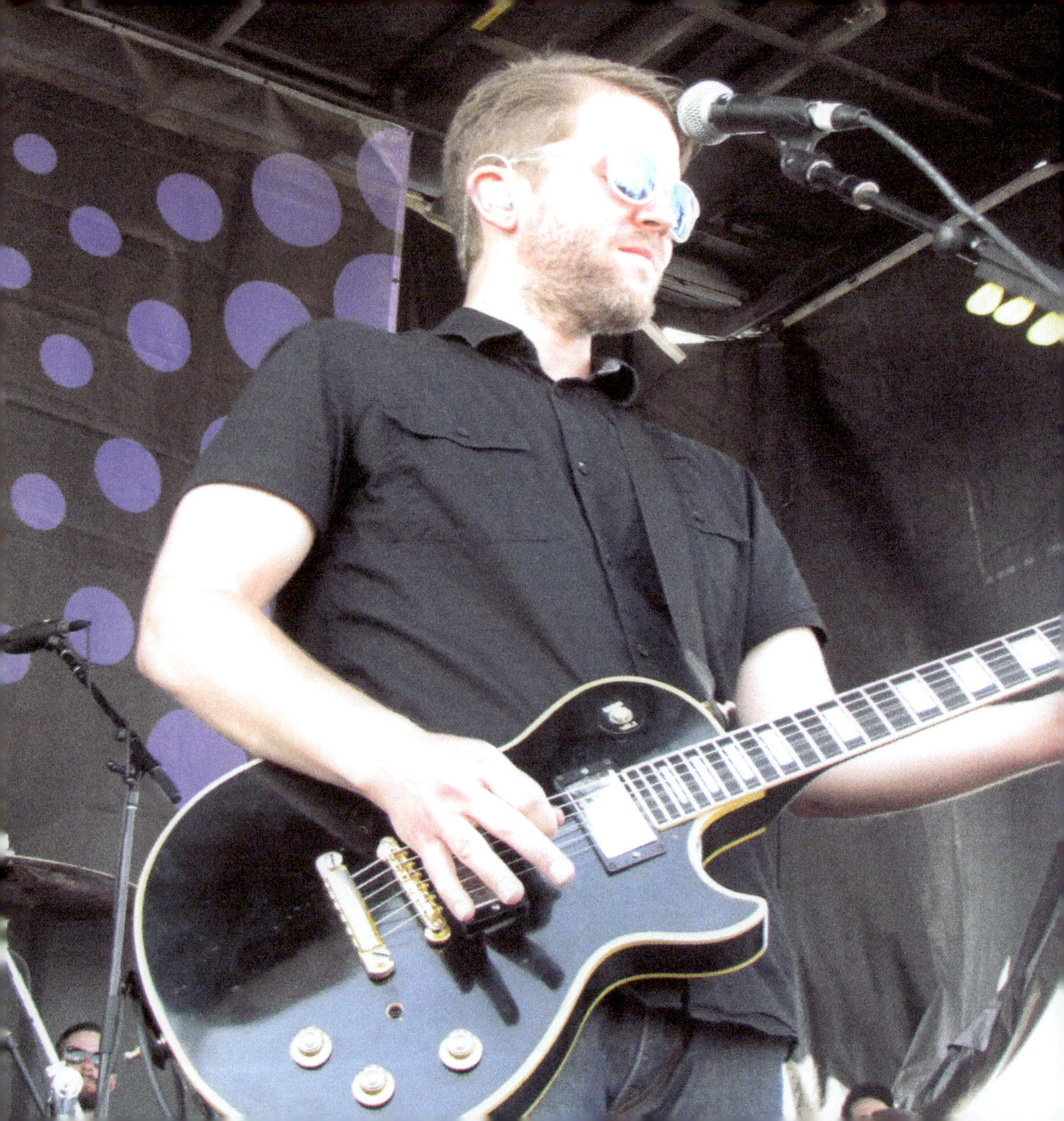

WHEN I GOT THE MUSIC, I GOT A PLACE TO GO

The legacy of the pop-punk/emo days go beyond the societal constraints of the Myspace-era, Hot Topic, studded belts and whatever other cliché comes to mind. If a boy or a girl broke your heart, well, the music was the place to go. I could recall countless nights I spent on Napster and Limewire just downloading music and talking to friends on AIM (AOL Instant Messenger).

The girl you like is in love with someone else? There's a song for that.

Are your parents getting divorced? There's a song for that.

Work sucks? There's a song for that.

Your best friend is moving away? There's a song for that.

You are an angst-filled teen angry at the world? There's a song for that.

There's a reason so many found comfort in these songs. There's a reason that those same feelings still resonate today with a new youth culture. While the original fans of this time are now in their thirties or older, the love for the music goes beyond the nostalgia. It was more than a mere instance in time, but a movement that fostered an idea of community, of family, that connected people all over the globe. As the Internet and social media were rising around this time, it was a perfect storm of synchronicity to make loners feel less alone, make pop-punk kids feel validated, and helped show that counter culture could actually be part of popular culture.

The songs speak to us in a way rap, rock, and soulless corporate radio pop don't.

Like a family heirloom, music can be passed down from older generations. The adults who grew up in the scene now bring their kids to the shows, thus introducing a new youth to the soundtrack of their parent's musical upbringing.

"Music mends broken hearts" was one of the slogans associated with Absolutepunk.net, which was one of the mega-sites responsible for branding this music beyond just message boards.

"Music mends broken hearts."

Couldn't have said it better myself.

A NEW AMERICANA

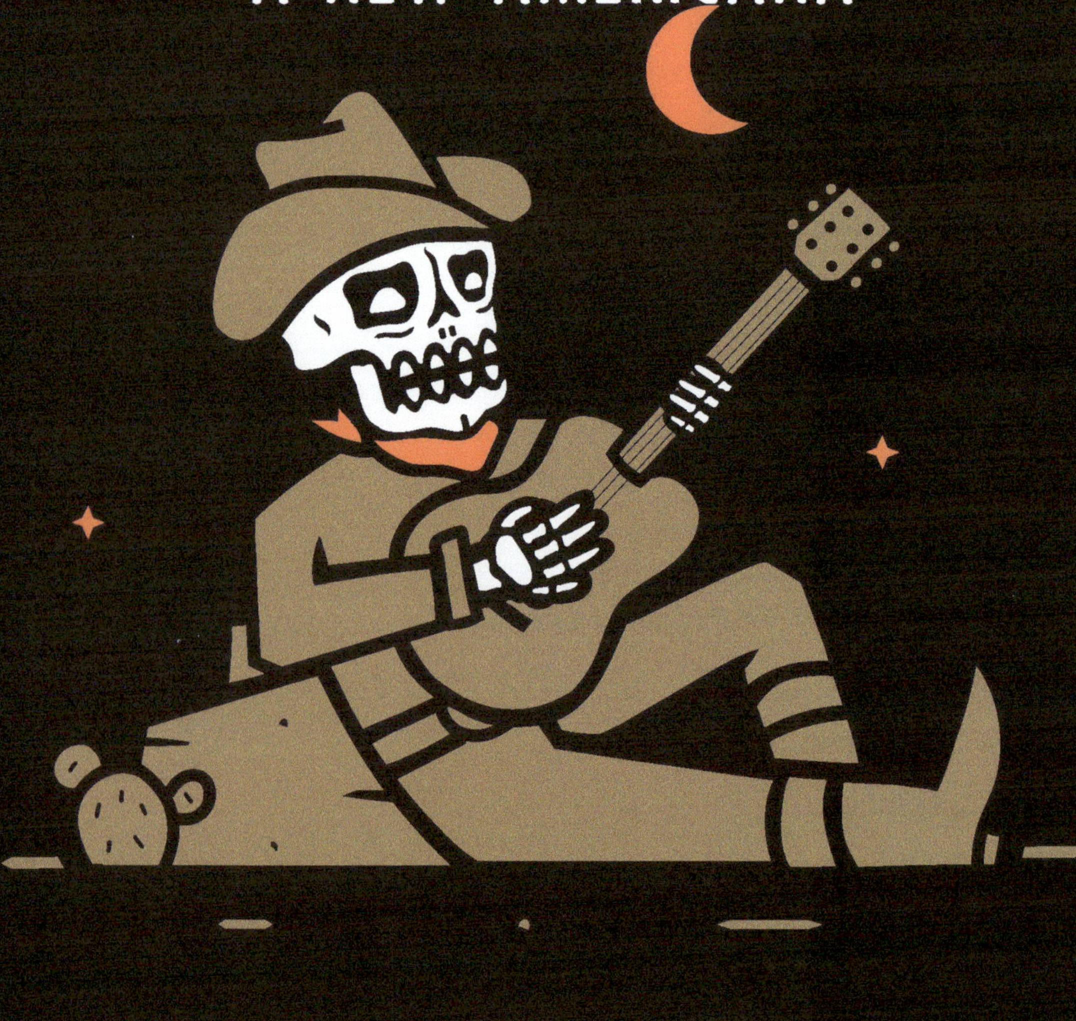

Americana represents the culture and historical importance of the United States. Now, don't get this confused with nationalism, which is the promotion and support of a nation's interests to the detriment of other nations. Americana as a musical art form helped pave the way for contemporary pop culture.

Americana music was rich in its roots of folk, rock'n'roll, blues, blue grass, and R&B. Woody Guthrie ("This Land Is Your Land") was one of the first Western folk singers to weave the idea of betterment and the American condition. This helped pave the way for American blue-collar anthems from Bruce Springsteen, and protest music eventually made popular by acts as big as Rage Against The Machine.

Rock'n' roll was always supposed to be rebellious, and that rebellion didn't stop with the waves of grunge, metal, alt-rock, indie, reggae, ska, punk, pop-punk and emo. What was being rebelled against may have changed, but the general spirit was there.

When Black Flag sang "Rise Above" it wasn't just a song lyric, but it was a call to action for the apathetic, angry, tired, and poor to act. Now, you can point to the covered musical movements here, and see commonalities:

- Distrust of establishment

- Opposing societal norms

- A romanticism revival

- Strife

- Grief

- Anger

- Pain

- Hope

- Belonging

- Growing up

- Giving up

- Storytelling

- Romance and romantic troubles

The settings, time, and antagonists may have changed through the years, but emotion has remained the same. All music is emotive by nature, so when a musical genre is classified as "emo" it is truly a vague qualifier. When looking at the big picture of the struggling artist and the strife of human condition, it can seem strange to constrict the emo genre to a subculture of post-hardcore rock.

Can you see these similar characteristics in other musical genres like country and hip-hop? Of course. Hip-hop specifically can be raw and emotional, especially when looking at political leaning acts like N.W.A and Public Enemy. It's not that far-fetched to equate hip-hop and punk/rock'n'roll, as similar houses on the same street.

Music is ultimately a universal language. The sounds, vibrations, energy and feeling elicit emotions intrinsically.

This is what helps connect people cross culturally, including bridging subculture to popular culture. The way music resonates allows scenes to exist in various cities all over the world.

THE FUTURE
FREAKS ME OUT

Currently, in 2019-2020, mainstream music is dominated by pop, hip-hop, and K-pop, while rock bands are finding it harder to make waves on the radio. The big rock bands that frequent the radio are acts like Twenty One Pilots and Imagine Dragons, which aren't exactly the hardest of musical bands. But rock music may have a resurgence to the youth of today from some unlikely sources. Hip-hop star Post Malone isn't afraid to cross genres, and some of his songs have both acoustic and electric guitars. In 2020, Post Malone made waves during the global pandemic of COVID-19 when he put together a live Nirvana cover set. The expansive, and impressive, Nirvana cover show also included blink-182's Travis Barker on drums, and overall gained rave reviews.

So, if hip-hop artists can help usher the younger generation to rock and punk music, then not all is lost.

Another rapper, Machine Gun Kelly, who was always a fan of rock and pop-punk, took a similar genre course correction. In 2020, he released *Tickets To My Downfall*, which was a rock/pop-punk record produced by Barker, who also drummed. Songs like "Bloody Valentine" and "Concerts For Aliens" were some of the best pop-punk songs in years. Pop-star Halsey also appeared on the song "Forget Me Too." She also references blink-182 in the song "Closer", which she made with mega-producers/pop act The Chainsmokers.

Upcoming artists nothing,nowhere. and Nascar Aloe are also mixing hip-hop and punk. The trend of mixing rap and rock isn't new, and you can see precursors to the movement in Ice T's band Body Count, which mixed hardcore, metal, and rap, and the supergroup The Transplants (Tim Armstrong, Travis Barker, and Skinhead Rob).

Now this is not to say rock music is dead, nor are the emo and pop-punk sub genres. The bands still do very well on tour, and chart high on Billboard and Spotify plays, but may not get the radio play they once did. While radio still maintains its "power," it is dwindling due to steaming sources (Spotify, Soundcloud, Apple Music) emergence as a new powerhouse in the music industry. In 2020, blink-182 was nominated for an MTV VMA, and many popular songs from the emo heyday have become resurrected through YouTube reaction videos, memes, and other social media sensations.

In 2019, My Chemical Romance rocked the music world when it announced its reformation and return. Tickets to the band's entire North American tour sold out in just six hours. The tour, which would be the band's first in nine years, sold 228,600 tickets in that short time, according to Forbes.com.

NEW NOISE

The future of the scene seems to be in good hands, as the sound of the genre progresses just like initial punk rock did with bands like The Clash and The Damned.

Under the loosely interrupted emo tag, bands like Joyce Manor, The Dangerous Summer, Jetty Bones, Tigers Jaw, The Hotelier, Free Throw, Modern Baseball, The Front Bottoms, You Blew It!, Lemuria, and Hot Mulligan are carrying the torch just fine, and bringing in a new wave of kids.

Hardcore has evolved with bands like Touche Amore, who make the heavy sounds of the genre sound beautiful and emotive, while acts like Enter Shikari bring in electronic and arena rock elements. Knocked Loose, War On Women, Counter Parts, and Code Orange are keeping the genre aggressive.

Pop-punk isn't dead either, as bands such as The Wonder Years, The Menzingers, Knuckle Puck, Neck Deep, State Champs, PUP, Seaway, Hot Milk, and Direct Hit! continue on the subculture.

SCENE REPORT:
ARTISTS, PUBLICISTS AND INDUSTRY FOLK ON SOME OF THEIR BEST MEMORIES

"New Found Glory" (self-titled) - New Found Glory:

"Growing up when you're into punk and hard core, there are certain records like Rancid "Let's Go" and NOFX "Punk In Drublic" you have to have. There are certain records that are like a starter kit. And I feel that [self-titled album] has kind of gotten into that category.

What is cool about it, it is super raw sounding, especially compared to the stuff nowadays. It was recorded on analog tape, and it has no pro tools. When kids get into pop-punk now, they get into that record."

-Chad Gilbert, New Found Glory

On seeing the Get Up Kids for the first time:

"The first time I saw The Get Up Kids was in 2001 when I bought tickets to see Green Day. I couldn't drive at the time, so I begged my friend to drive. I can't even remember what city it was, but it was a three and a half hour drive to catch any good band that would come near my small Midwest town.

I remember thinking, "who is this band?" while they played the song "Ten Minutes". Why was their backdrop logo a robot? Were they DJs? Why is everyone pushing each other?

I waited until we made it back to our small city, and I went to the 'cool' record store to buy it. It was called 'Stick It In Your Ear' and they had it. That was my first introduction to emo music, and I remember liking all their faster songs. I had to have my high school boyfriend break up with me before I liked anything else on that record.

Insert fifteen years, and I was asked to tour manage and do their sound, I was like, absolutely! Without even knowing how much they paid. I still can't believe sometimes that I worked for my teenage icons. What made things even better was that they are all beautiful generous humans. I couldn't ask for a greater group of people to be on tour with and work for in the future!"

-Jenny Douglas (Former sound, tour manager for New Found Glory, Senses Fail, The Get Up Kids)

The Get Up Kids on Vagrant scene:

"Well, at the time, the Alkaline Trio, Saves The Day, Dashboard [Confessional], and us all had the same manager and booking agent and beyond that we were all drinking buddies before we were label mates. The Anniversary were from Lawrence and Hot Rod Circuit toured with us more times than I can count. Again, drinking buddies."

-Matt Pryor, The Get Up Kids

Importance of "From Under The Cork Tree":

"Hate them or love them, Fall Out Boy is one of the most influential bands of the scene, whether one wants to admit it or not. "From Under The Cork Tree" (2005) is an album that took the scene above ground. Though the album was Fall out Boy's sophomore record ("Evening Out With Your Ex Girlfriend", who?), it was the band's first major label debut. The album propelled the previously lesser-known band to mainstream radio success, and would serve as the band's first chart topping album (No.9 on the Billboard Top 200).

At the time, punk pop was not prevalent in the Top 40 pop driven radio spectrum. "Sugar We're Going Down," the first single off "From Under The Cork Tree," without a doubt changed that, and introduced a new level of inclusivity to the music industry. Additionally, it would see a scene band being nominated for a Grammy in the 'Best New Artist' category in 2006. Fall Out Boy set a precedence for the scene with this album paving way for the success of acts like Paramore and Panic! At The Disco. Fall Out Boy made being seemingly uncool, be cool. The outsiders were suddenly at the cool kids' table due to the success of this album.

For me, personally, Fall Out Boy was a band who got me into music. Growing up, I mostly listened to what my friends listened to; I was a sheep. I did not have a real musical identity. I will never forget the day that I saw the music video for "Sugar We're Going Down" on Fuse TV's countdown. I was instantly hooked. It launched a world of music discovery for me. Not to mention, it helped me decide what industry I wanted to work in. FUTCT got this sheep out of the crowd."

-Michele Stephens, Epitaph Records tour publicist

On playing the late-night TV circuit:

"We started getting invited to play on all the big late-night shows, we even did SNL, which was such a milestone for us! I remember when we did Letterman we wanted to do something crazy, so we decided we would smash our gear at the end of the song. I'm pretty sure the whole stage crew was so bummed, and we never got asked to play his show again! For as much shit as we took for 'selling out' the scene back then, we knew how many young fans we were turning into rock music fans and we focused on delivering a message of hope to them. MTV and late-night shows were great opportunities, and we were thankful for the outlet."

-Billy Martin, Good Charlotte

The success of clothing brands like Atticus:

"Atticus saw that niche in the market and jumped all in. During those early emo years, Atticus sold more black T-shirts than any other youth brand in the

U.S., selling 30 to 40 thousand units of each design just in the U.S. each season, and when you add in international sales it was ridiculous. One of the top selling pieces during that time was the Atticus dead bird polo. Again, during that time preppy Ralph Lauren and Izod polos were everywhere, which gave us the idea for the logo before we started. The idea of a dead bird patch on a polo couldn't be further from the horse jockey, leaping tiger, or alligator polos, but at the same time it was right on point for the trend."

-Dylan Anderson, founder and brand manager of Atticus Clothing, and current brand manager for Hi My Name Is Mark.

On being in a female-fronted act:

"In some ways, being a woman in the pop scene was like being thrown to a pack wolves dressed in skinny jeans and crewneck sweatshirts. I've made some of the closest friends of my life, and I've said it before, but you'll never feel as close to someone as when you're on the eighth hour of an impossible drive and you're in the desert and it's four in the morning. I still get nostalgic for the crunch of leaves on that first fall tour of the season, when you step out of the van in New England, but there's always been this sense of loneliness. I don't know if everyone feels it, but being the only woman in a group of 35 or so men can feel isolating. It's fun, but it's lonely. It took me a while to *notice, but no matter how hard I tried to fit in, I always felt a minor—but distinct—sense of otherness.*

I believe that over the years the large lack of gender parity subtly taught us that women were the subject of songs, not the people who get to write them. We were taught that women don't get to take up the same amount of space, but it's just a self-perpetuating lie created by our culture. In the music industry, you don't get a platform unless you fight for it—and we can fight for it. I'm happy to see it changing more in recent years. It only takes one woman with a guitar to inspire a little girl – to teach her that her voice is important and just as loud as every other heartbroken man singing about his ex. In a genre fueled by aggression, we can still find tenderness. Or we can channel our rage. We're human, too."

-Mariel Loveland [Candy Hearts/Best Ex]

On working at Alternative Press during the boom:

"Being entrenched for the rise of bands like Fall Out Boy, My Chemical Romance and Taking Back Sunday was exciting, and being able to finagle some of my personal favorites onto our cover (such as Against Me!, the Gaslight Anthem and Manchester Orchestra) was always fun – even if those issues were some of our all-time worst sellers. There's no accounting for

taste, I suppose!

The scene eventually mutated into a bunch of terrible, faceless metalcore and pop-punk bands, but for a few short years, there was this strange mixture of art and commerce that created a ton of incredible music and created a culture that still thrives till this day. Would I have liked it to happen a few years earlier with bands like Braid, the Get Up Kids and the Promise Ring? Sure, but at least it got Jimmy Eat World a platinum record!

-Scott Heisel, former writer/editor at Alternative Press magazine

The blog scene:

"Having a modest, medium-sized website in the late 2000s to 2015 was pretty exciting—despite the bread and butter of our website being hip-hop and indie-rock. Covering Warped Tours and the punk bands at festivals like Austin City Limits, Fun Fun Fun Fest, Free Press Summer Fest and Day for Night was pretty essential for us, if not for the nostalgia.

Growing up on this stuff was a huge part of all of our lives, and building relationships with the record labels, promoters and the festivals allowed us to cover some of our favorite bands regularly, namely Every Time I

Die, Thrice, Coheed and Cambria, New Found Glory and plenty more. In a post-website coverage world, it's fun to see the evolution of the genre and what newer bands are doing, even if you're not totally into it. What's even better is seeing the bands influenced by that era of music that are growing in popularity today—your Wonder Years, Tigers Jaws and the like—bands that truly capture the essence of old influences and sounds to creating more modernized music."

-Roshan Bhatt, co-founder of weworemasks.com

On Warped Tour Life:

"Warped Tour was about a community unit. Discovery of life, music, difference and similarities. Kevin Lyman did an amazing job finding a team that commanded respect and ran the tour seamlessly. It's a tough, sweaty tour and it takes grit to survive and succeed. Nothing is handed to you without your contributing."

-Bethany Watson, Warped Tour Press Manager

A DAY IN THE LIFE OF A TOUR MANAG

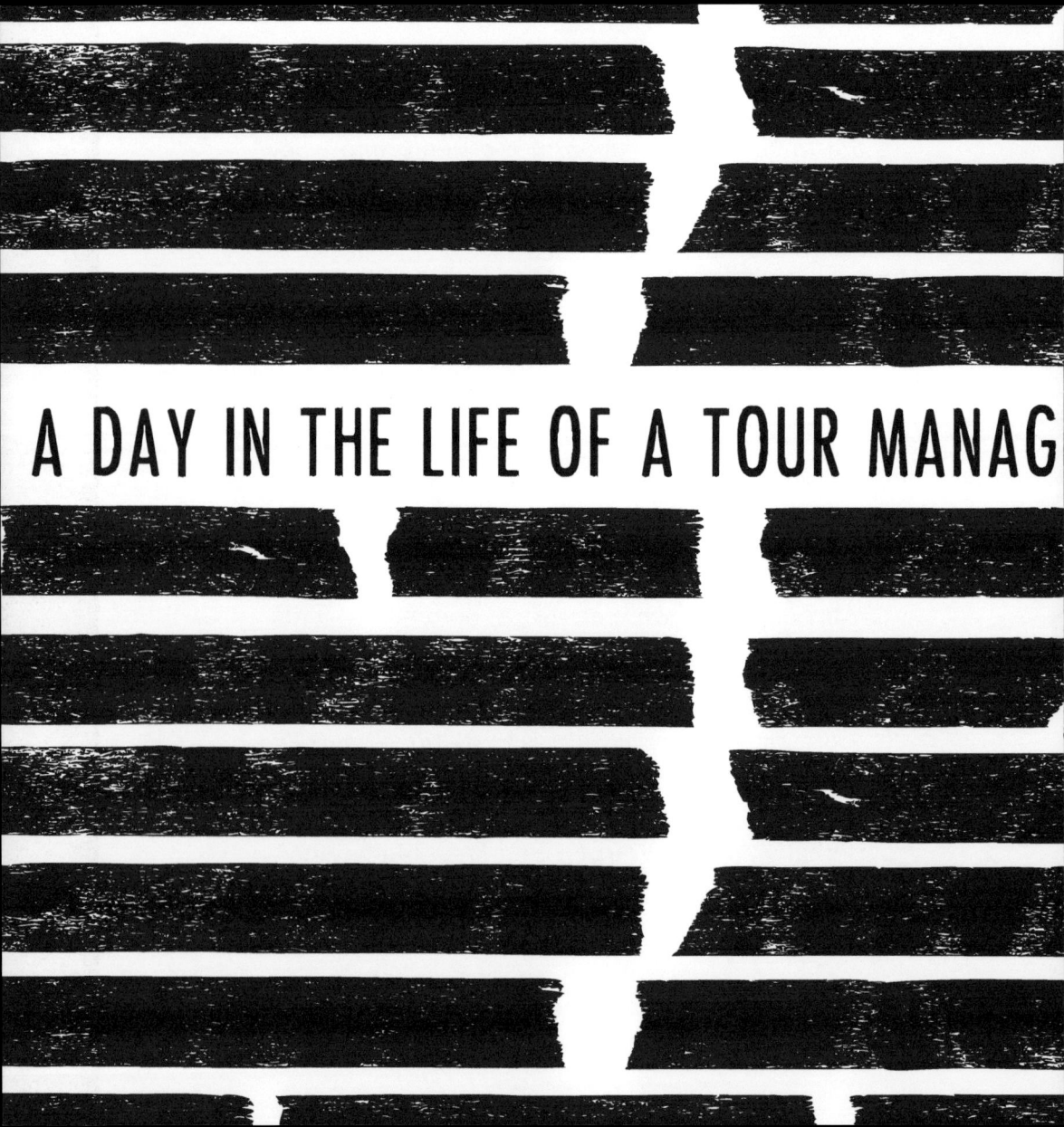

Jeff "Rhino" Neumann does many jobs during the week, like being the head tech at Soundcheck Houston, and building drums kits at Hendrix Drums, but the weekends bring his most important duty. He is the tour manager of legendary punk band the Descendents.

Neumann and the Descendents have been embarking on weekend treks all around the world since the band returned to semi-full-time touring, which is a luxury for established acts like the pop-punk pioneers. Neumann was glad to be home; the show for the night was at the House of Blues in his hometown of Houston, Texas.

The day started in typical Descendents fashion: coffee. Then a visit to Custom Drum Concepts (his original drum-building company at the time) where Neumann checked on some custom orders before loading gear with Soundcheck tech Donnie Reyes (the original drummer of Fenix TX). Once arriving at the House Of Blues for load in, Neumann did the work of a whole team, setting up the stage and paying meticulous attention to the drum setup. Neumann's business of crafting drums comes in handy working with punk drum maestro Bill Stevenson. Stevenson is an intimidating enigma; part drum legend à la Black Flag, part musical technician, and part loveable teddy bear—once he lets his guard down. Setting up the drums for him is a job itself, but Neumann is always up to task.

"He does so many things; he does stuff with the drum tuning and the structure of drums, but he's doing like 85,000 other things too for us," said Stevenson.

Paper work and setlists were already done—some procedural processes done months in advance—which shows Neumann's keen attention to detail and professionalism.

"He's doing like six guys' jobs right now, and he keeps his mood together pretty good because you get thrown so many weird curve balls doing what he does. And has to learn an incredible amount of stuff like 'here, learn how to be a monitor manager!' and he's been absolutely fantastic," said guitarist Stephen Egerton.

Few bands could afford to just travel the world and play sold-out shows on the weekend, but for pop-punk's eldest statesman, shows like Houston's House Of Blues is a time to reconnect with acts such as Riverboat Gamblers and Scott Reynolds from ALL.

"That was a very good plan we put in place a few years ago, but we want to try to play more and more than just playing a weekend here and a weekend there," said vocalist Milo Aukerman. "It's kind of nice to play these shows, like it's a special occasion, or a reunion of sorts."

Neumann grew up on the Westside of Houston

in the Memorial area, and attended Straftord High School before beginning tours in 1998 with another Houston alum, Fenix TX. Since then, Neumann has an impressive resume in punk and rock, working with Bad Religion, Sparta, Bouncing Souls, blink-182, Avenged Sevenfold, All American Rejects, Rise Against, Tenacious D, and others. In 2011, he began working with the Descendents, which was an instant career highlight.

"That is still insane to me at times," Neumann said. "These guys are the most down to earth band I have had the pleasure of working with. It really doesn't feel like work; it's like hanging out with friends every other weekend."

Photo (p110-111): Jeff "Rhino" Neumann wears many hats for the DESCENDENTS including drum tech for the legendary Bill Stevenson.

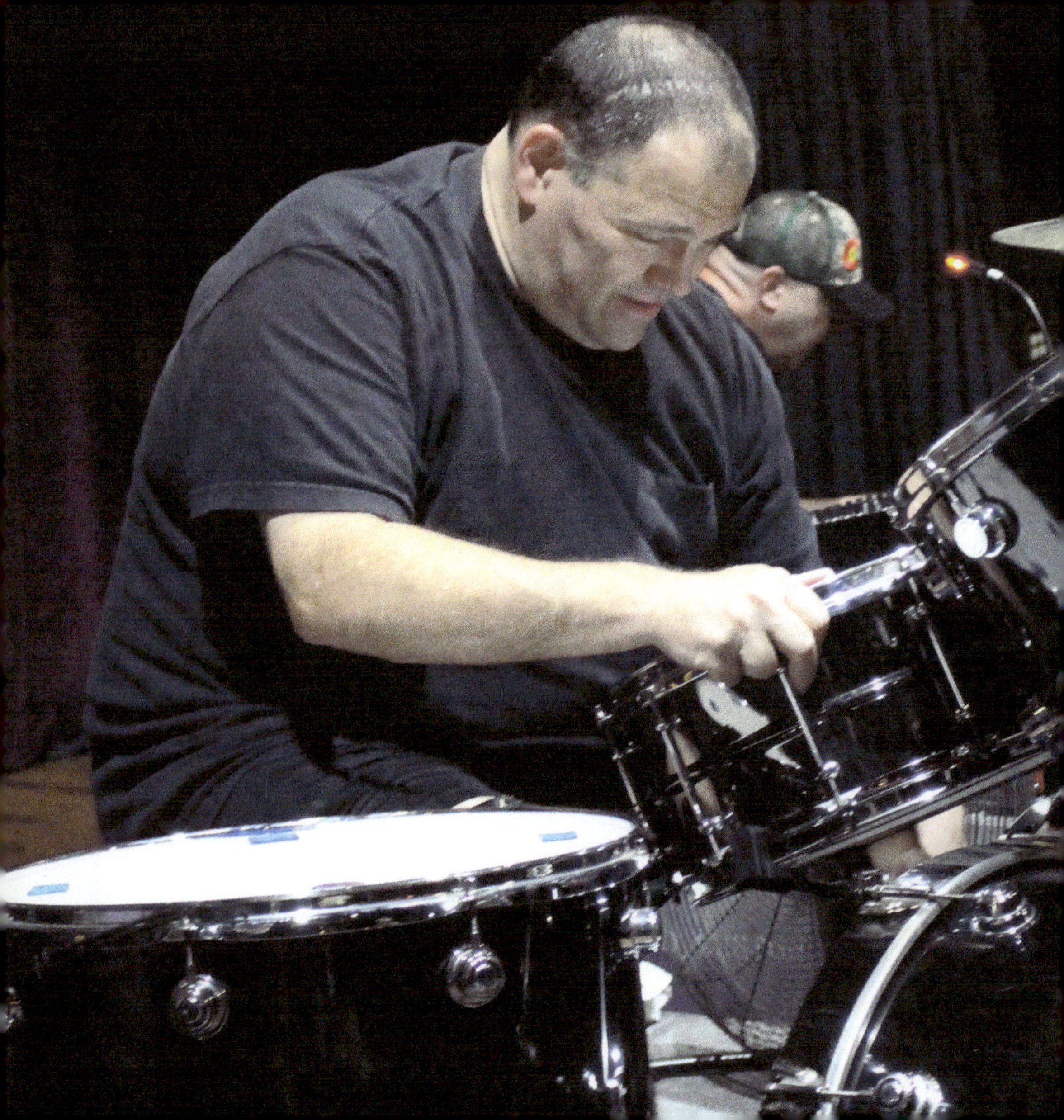

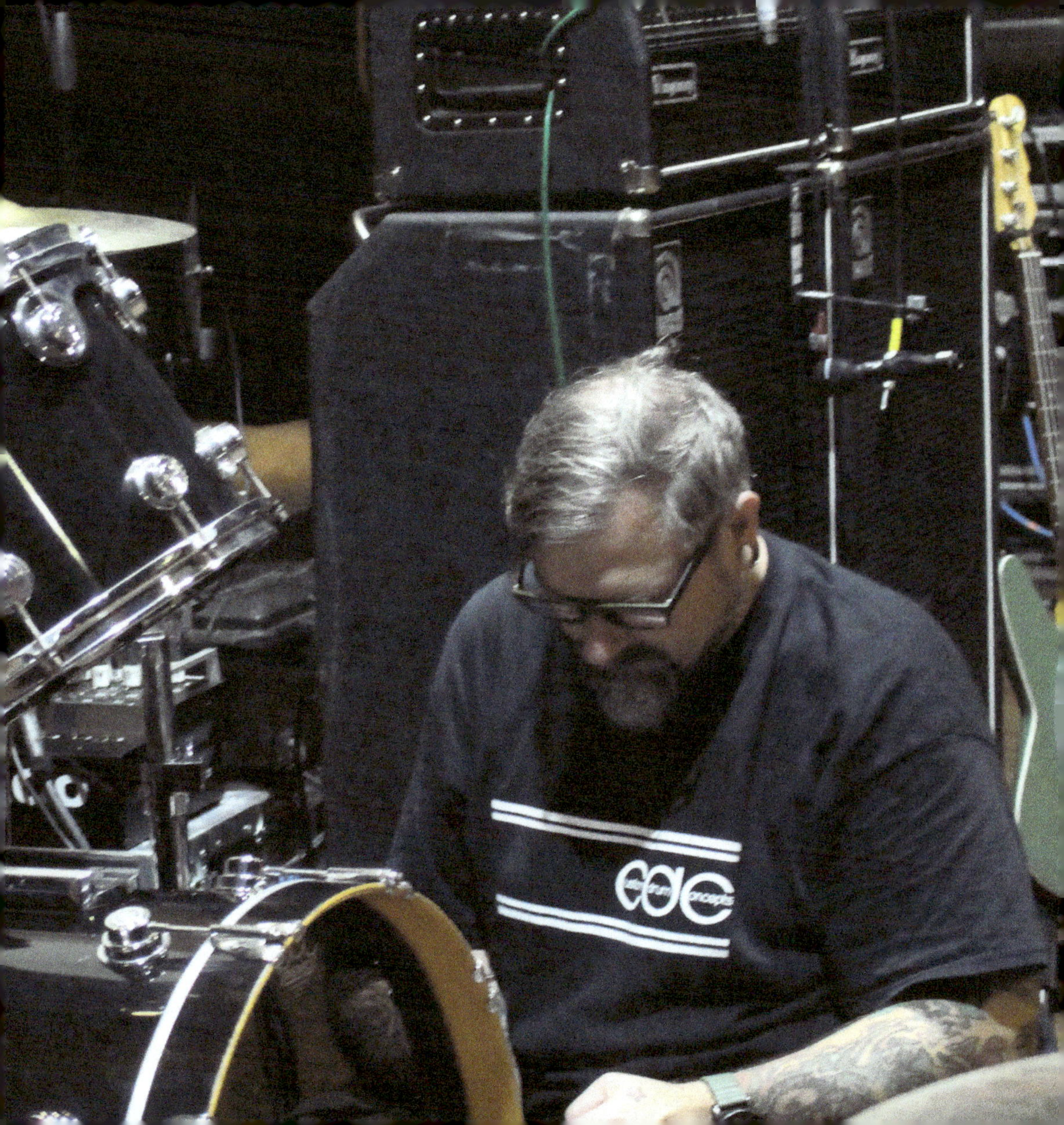

ULTIMATE PLAYLIST

ALL-AMERICAN REJECTS - The Last Song

ALL-AMERICAN REJECTS - Swing, Swing

AFI - The Leaving Song Pt. 2

AFI - Miss Murder

AFI - Girl's Not Grey

ANTI-FLAG - Turncoat

ALLISTER - Scratch

ALLISTER - Somewhere on Fullerton

ALKALINE TRIO - Private Eye

ALKALINE TRIO - My Friend Peter

THE USED - The Taste Of Ink

THE USED - A Box Full of Sharp Objects

BAYSIDE - Duality

BAYSIDE - Devotion and Desire

BLINK-182 - Dammit

BLINK-182 - The Rock Show

BOX CAR RACER - There Is

BRAND NEW - Sic Transit Gloria...Glory Fades

BAD RELIGION - Let Them Eat War

THE STARTING LINE - Up And Go

THE STARTING LINE - Best Of Me

FUGAZI - Waiting Room

RISE AGAINST - Swing Life Away

STRIKE ANYWHERE - To the World

THRICE - Deadbolt

THRICE - Under A Killing Moon

THURSDAY - Understanding in A Car Crash

THURSDAY - Signals Over The Air

ANGELS & AIRWAVES - The Adventure

BANE - Some Came Running

H20 - What Happened?

PARAMORE - Misery Business

PARAMORE - That's What You Get

PARAMORE - For a Pessimist, I'm Pretty Optimistic

FALL OUT BOY - Sugar, We're Going Down

FALL OUT BOY - Tell That Mick He Just Made My List Of Things To Do Today

THE GET UP KIDS - Holiday

THE GET UP KIDS - Action and Action

JIMMY EAT WORLD - A Praise Chorus

JIMMY EAT WORLD - The Middle

BOWING FOR SOUP - Girls All The Bad Guys Want

BOWLING FOR SOUP - 1985

GOOD CHARLOTTE - The Anthem

GOOD CHARLOTTE - Riot Girl

AGAINST ME - I Was A Teenage Anarchist

THE MENZINGERS - I Don't Wanna Be An Asshole Anymore

JOYCE MANOR - Heart Tattoo

BOUNCING SOULS - Lean On Sheena

THE NEW AMSTERDAMS - Turn Out the Light

NOFX - Franco Un-American

NOFX - Separation of Church and Skate

MEST - Cadillac

MXPX - My Life Story

AT THE DRIVE-IN - One Armed Scissor

CURSIVE - The Recluse

CIRCA SURVIVE - Meet Me in Montauk

RANCID - Fall Back Down

REEL BIG FISH - Sell Out

PIEBALD - American Hearts

RIDDLIN KIDS - Crazy

YELLOWCARD - Ocean Avenue

BLOC PARTY - Banquet

DEATH CAB FOR CUTIE - Soul Meets Body

THE PROMISE RING - Why Did Ever We Meet

RELIENT K - Who I Am Hates Who I've Been

SPARTA - Cut Your Ribbon

COHEED AND CAMBRIA - A Favor House Atlantic

REGGIE AND THE FULL EFFECT - Congratulations Smack and Katy

HOT WATER MUSIC - Remedy

SLICK SHOES - Once Again

SAVES THE DAY - Shoulder To The Wheel

SAVES THE DAY - At Your Funeral

TAKING BACK SUNDAY - Cute Without The E (Cut From The Team)

TAKING BACK SUNDAY - Set Phasers To Stun

NEW FOUND GLORY - Hit Or Miss

NEW FOUND GLORY - My Friends Over You

MOTION CITY SOUNDTRACK - My Favorite Accident

MOTION CITY SOUNDTRACK - Everything Is Alright

CANDY HEARTS - I Miss You

+44 - Lycanthrope

MIDTOWN - Just Rock And Roll

ALL TIME LOW - Weightless

ALL TIME LOW - Dear Maria, Count Me In

THE GASLIGHT ANTHEM - The 59 Sound

THE GASLIGHT ANTHEM - Drive

GREEN DAY - Welcome To Paradise

GREEN DAY - Longview

A DAY TO REMEMBER - Since U Been Gone

THE LAWRENCE ARMS - 100 Resolutions

CUTE IS WHAT WE AIM FOR - There's A Class For This

SOMETHING CORPORATE - Punk Rock Princess

FURTHER SEEMS FOREVER - The Sound

HOT ROD CIRCUIT - The Pharmacist

THE ANNIVERSARY - D in Detroit

LESS THAN JAKE - The Science Of Selling Your Self Short

THE MIGHTY MIGHTY BOSSTONES - The Impression That I Get

MONEEN - If Tragedy's Appealing, Then Disaster's An Addiction

ARMOR FOR SLEEP - The Truth About Heaven

NORTHSTAR - American Living

RIVAL SCHOOLS - On Vacations

REFUSED - New Noise

RUFIO - Above Me

RUFIO - Still

TSUNAMI BOMB - Take the Reins

HOMEGROWN - Give It Up

PRETTY GIRLS MAKE GRAVES - Speakers Push Air

GLASSJAW - Ape Dos Mil

TOUCHÉ AMORÉ - Flowers And You

HEAD AUTOMATICA - Beating Heart Baby

SAY ANYTHING - Wow! I Can Get Sexual, Too

MY CHEMICAL ROMANCE - I'm Not Okay (I Promise)

MY CHEMICAL ROMANCE - Helena

SUM41 - Fat Lip

SUM 41 - Summer

THE MOVIELIFE - Jamestown

THE MOVIELIFE - Hand Grenade

DASHBOARD CONFESSIONAL - Hands Down

DASHBOARD CONFESSIONAL - Screaming Infidelities

AUDIO KARATE - Nintendo '89

PANIC AT THE DISCO - I Write Sins, Not Tragedies

SUGARCULT - Memory

THE ATARIS - San Dimas High School Football Rules

SIMPLE PLAN - Shut Up

SIMPLE PLAN - I'd Do Anything

RX BANDITS - Analog Boy

THE POSTAL SERVICE - Such Great Heights

THE JULIANA THEORY - If I Told You This Was Killing Me, Would You Stop

BRAID - A Dozen Roses

FENIX TX - O_Bleek

FENIX TX - All My Fault

THE FRONT BOTTOMS - Skeleton

THE EARLY NOVEMBER - Ever So Sweet

THE FORMAT - The First Single

AMERICAN FOOTBALL - Never Meant

CAP'N'JAZZ - Little League

HEY MERCEDES - A-List Actress

WEEZER - Why Bother?

WEEZER - Buddy Holly

HAWTHORNE HEIGHTS - Ohio Is For Lovers

STORY OF THE YEAR - Until The Day I Die

FINCH - What It Is To Burn

FOUR YEAR STRONG - It Must Really Suck To Be Four Year Strong Right Now

MODERN BASEBALL - Your Graduation

SENSES FAIL - Bloody Romance

MATCHBOX ROMANCE - The Greatest Fall (Of All Time)

WE THE KINGS - Check Yes, Juliet

BOYS LIKE GIRLS - The Great Escape

JAWBREAKER - Jet Black

JAWBREAKER - Want

JETS TO BRAZIL - Chinatown

THE WONDER YEARS - Passing Through A Screen Door

Don't like the list? There's plenty of songs missing, so please feel free to complain on the internet in early 2000s (and current social media) fashion.

TOP PUNK SONGS OF THE ERA

"Hit Or Miss" - New Found Glory: If you had to pick one song to define this era of pop-punk, you can't go wrong with choosing the forever enduring "Hit Or Miss."

"Talking" - Descendents: The pioneers of pop-punk returned to school the new school in with "Talking" off of 2004's "Cool To Be You."

"The Anthem" - Good Charlotte: The aptly-named track was off of Good Charlotte's hit-producing "The Young and the Hopeless."

"Private Eye" - Alkaline Trio: Alkaline Trio showed that pop-punk can have a darker aesthetic . "Private Eye" is a perfect mix of the band's ability to capture catchy with brooding.

"Sugar, We're Going Down" - Fall Out Boy: Fall Out Boy's heavy sugary-hook leanings, and this hit song helped make them one of the biggest bands in the world.

"Ocean Avenue" - Yellowcard: Fun fact: Yellowcard was the only "pop-punk" band to incorporate a violin. "Ocean Avenue" helped the band to be easily embraced by the MTV audience.

"The Rock Show" - blink-182: The perfect pop-punk summer anthem written as an ode to the Ramones, and the Warped Tour.

"O'Bleek" - Fenix TX: This rare gem off of Drive Thru

Records' "Welcome to the Family" compilation, shows the 2000s era of pop-punk at its best; catchy, fast and fun.

"A Praise Chorus" - Jimmy Eat World: While "The Middle" and "Sweetness" made this Arizona emo powerhouse a modern rock radio household name, "A Praise Chorus" was Jimmy Eat World at its finest.

"Jamestown" - The Movielife: The Movielife combined all the best aspects of the Long Island scene in this darker track.

"Stuck in America" - Sugarcult: You want to get out of your town and make something happen? That notion became a pop-punk cliche' before "Stuck In America" hit.

"Fat Lip" - Sum 41: "Fat Lip" was an instant crossover hit to bridge the gap between MTV, and the Warped Tour.

"Somewhere On Fullerton" - Allister: Allister was one of the better Drive Thru bands, and "Somewhere on Fullerton" was a defining song for the label, and its history.

"Analog Boy" - RX Bandits: A little of The Police, a hint of ska and a lot of simple pop-punk riffs made "Analog Boy" a memorable one.

"At Your Funeral" - Saves The Day: "At Your Funeral" was a glimpse into the future direction of the band with a nice nod to the band's emo/pop-punk past.

"In This Diary" - This Ataris: Kris Roe's reflective lyrics and style came to life on this track that helped these pop-punk veterans get some mainstream love.

"Nintendo 89" - Audio Karate: "Nintendo 89" was one of the more anthemic and memorable songs of the 2000s, despite not getting as much exposure as its peers did.

"Above Me" - Rufio: With intricate guitars, breakneck speed, and crisp musicianship Rufio was able to gain respect from other metal-leaning punk acts like Strung Out, and "Above Me" introduced a new crop of pop-punk kids to the faster, skate style.

"Cute Without the 'E' (Cut From The Team)" - Taking Back Sunday: A seminal favorite from the time, these emo rockers showed off some nice pop-punk chops.

"Up And Go" - The Starting Line: The Starting Line always was first in line in terms of being the safest of the mall bands, but "Up And Go" is a peppy pop-rock jam that will stick in your head like the gum at the bottom of your Vans.

FILM GUIDE

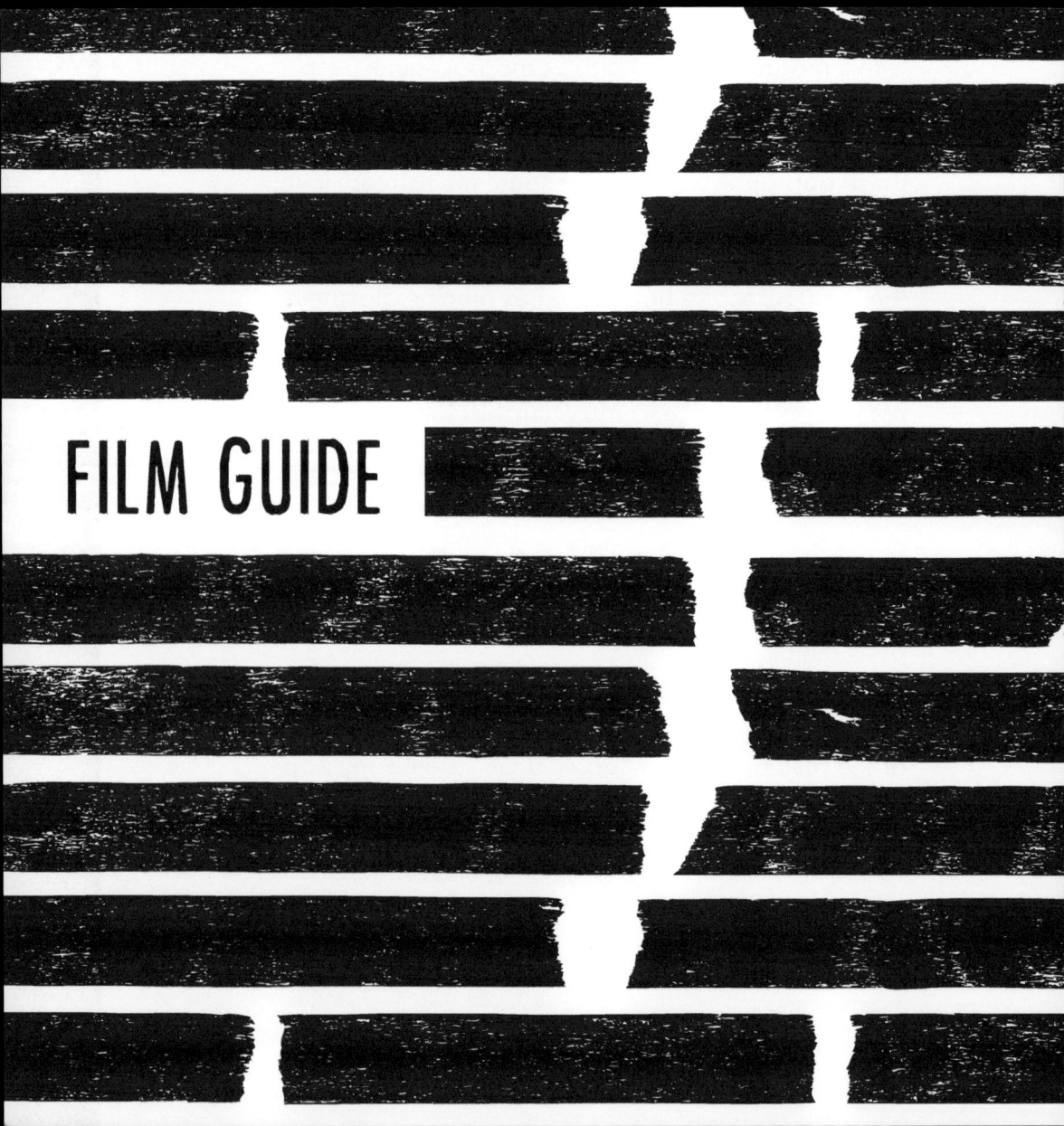

The Other F Word

Riding in Vans with Boys

Pick It Up! Ska in the '90s

Filmage: The Story of DESCENDENTS/ALL

New Found Glory: The Story So Far

Alkaline Trio - The Show Must Go Off!: Halloween At The Metro

blink-182 - The Urethra Chronicles (I and II)

Don't Break Down: A Film About Jawbreaker

Turn It Around: The Story of East Bay Punk

Paramore - The Final Riot

TOP COMPILATIONS

Welcome To The Family-Drive Thru Records

Atticus: ... Dragging The Lake

Vagrant; Another Year On The Streets (Vol.3)

Rock Against Bush Vol.1 (Fat Wreck Chords)

Punk-O-Rama 4 (Straight Outta The Pit), Epitaph Records

Tony Hawk's Pro Skater 2 Soundtrack

Saddle Creek 50

Warped Tour 2002 Tour Compilation

GLOSSARY

Pop-punk - Sub-genre that incorporates more of a melodic style of punk.

Emo - Emotive music with emphasis on expressive emotions.

Skate-punk - Southern California style of fast, and melodic punk.

Drive-Thru Records - Label launched by the Reines siblings that helped popularize the pop-punk and emo sound in the early to mid 2000s.

Indefinite Hiatus - When a band announces a "break."

Vans Warped Tour - Long-running music, skate, and lifestyle tour that helped launch careers of acts like No Doubt, Eminem, Katy Perry, blink-182, Rancid, NOFX, etc.

Absolutepunk.net - Popular website/online music community that promoted artists, and helped many bands reach new levels of popularity. Now called chorus.fm.

Myspace - Early social networking/ social media website that allowed fans, and bands to interact.

Headliner - Band that closes the show/ is placed atop the marquee.

Napster - One of the first popular websites to

download music.

TRL - MTV show "Total Request Live" that included viewers voting for the music videos to be played that day.

Epitaph - One of the largest independent labels started by Bad Religion's Brett Gurewitz.

Alternative Press - Print magazine that featured alternative rock, pop-punk, punk, and emo music.

Scene - Youth subculture of music, fashion, and hairstyles during the 2000s emo era.

Ska - Music with origins in Caribbean that would later combine reggae, rocksteady, and elements of dance hall, punk, and blues.

Hard core - Sub-genre of punk, but harder, faster, and more aggressive in sound.

Post-punk - Sub-genre that deviated away from punk's rawness, and incorporated more new wave elements.

Screamo - Sub-genre of emo categorized by aggressive and Avant Garde moments.

Fest - Short for musical festival; large gathering of multiple bands, and artists.

Metalcore - Subset of metal that combines melodic

elements of metal, punk, and hard core.

ESSENTIAL ALBUMS

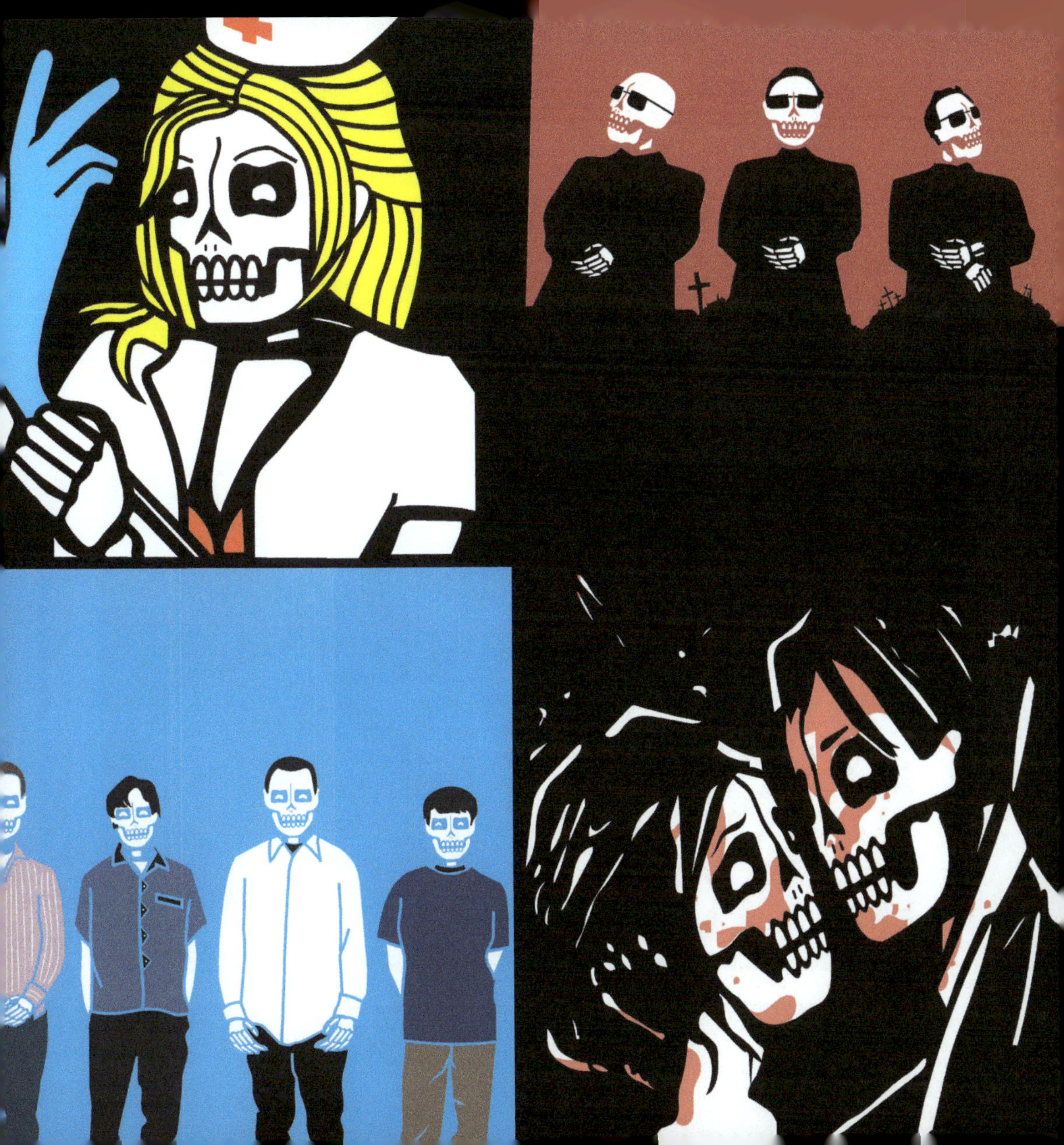

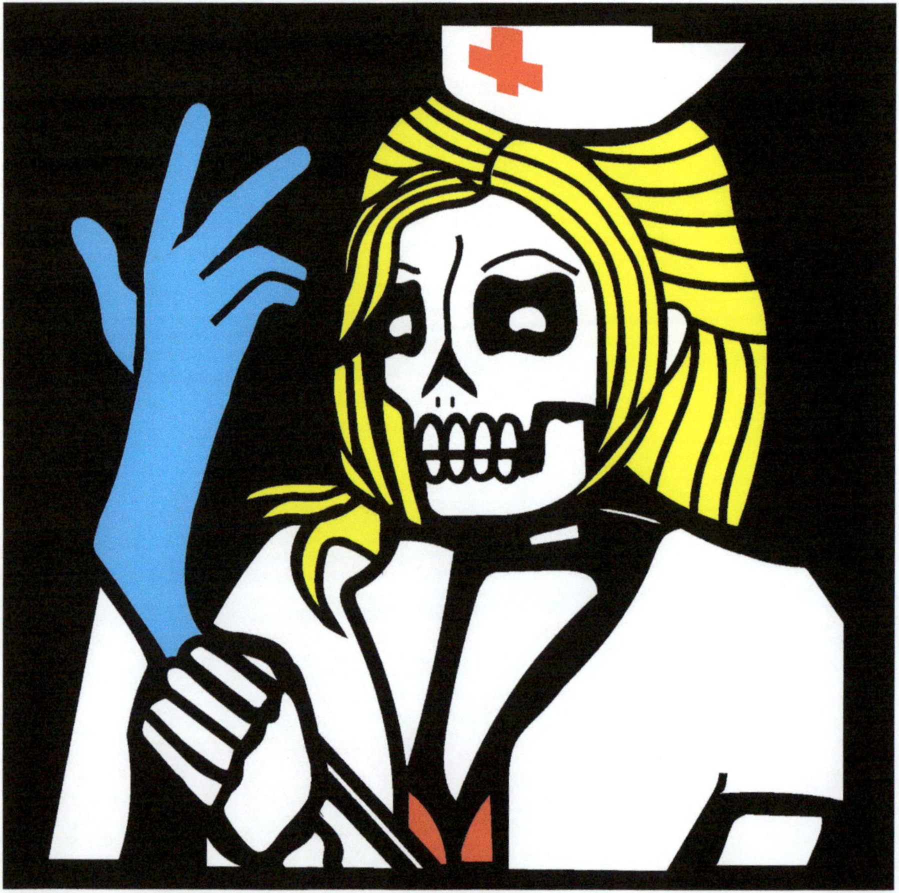

ENEMA OF THE STATE
BLINK—182

Enema Of The State is one of the biggest records of the 1990s, and one of the most influential albums of all time. This album propelled the band from punk-rock prowess to being a household name of super-stardom status. *Enema Of The State* is bratty, angsty and full of huge pop-punk choruses that made blink mainstays on MTV and radio. Ultimately, *Enema Of The State* remains a beloved album that transcended the genre of pop-punk.

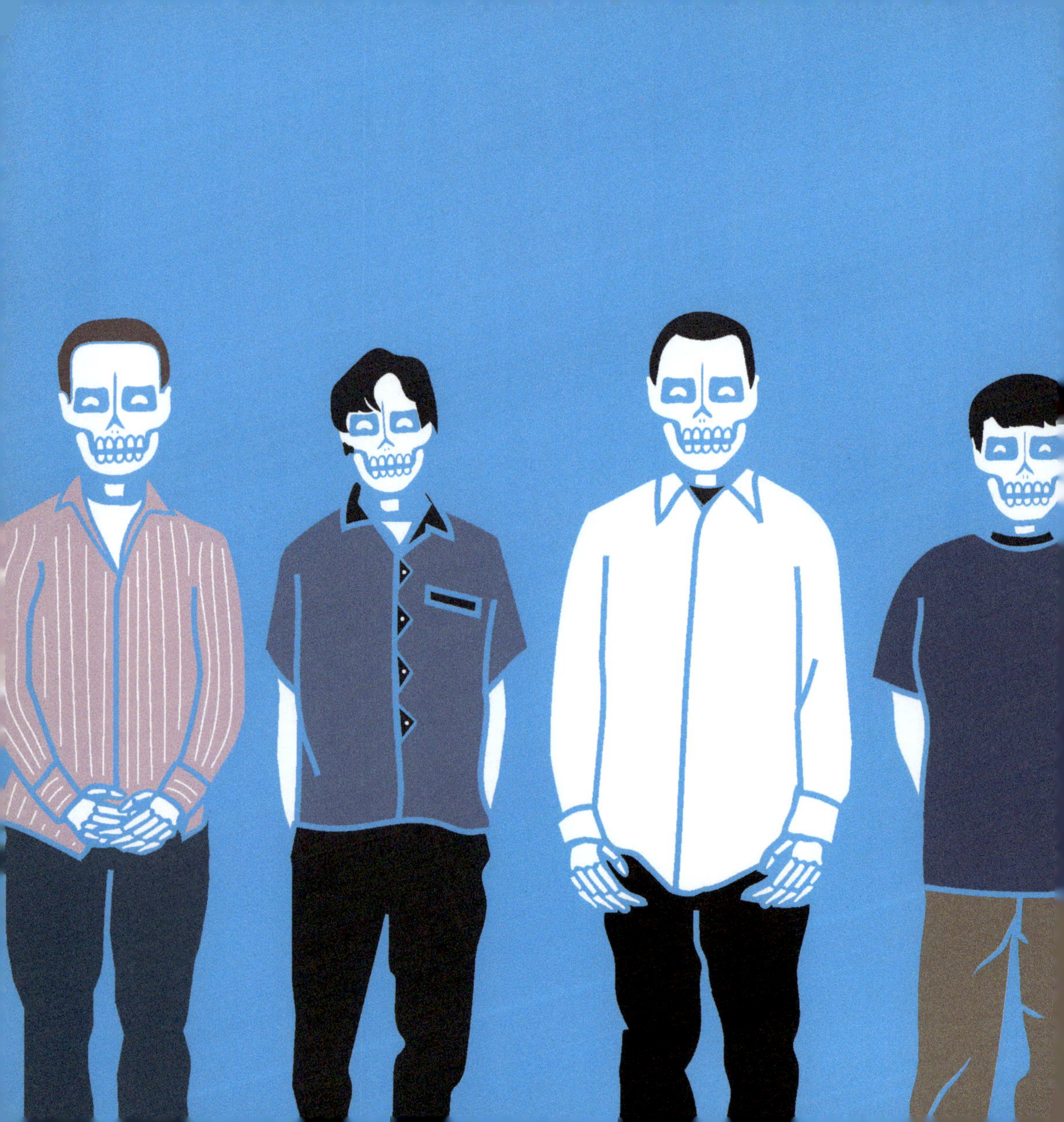

THE BLUE ALBUM
WEEZER

Not generally considered an "emo" album, Weezer's early work was important to set the stage for rock that was to come. One of the best albums from one of the best eras of alternative music, the record commonly referred to as *The Blue Album*, helped capture the voice of the 1990s generation. The underdog aesthetic and the garage band vibes set the standards for "emo."

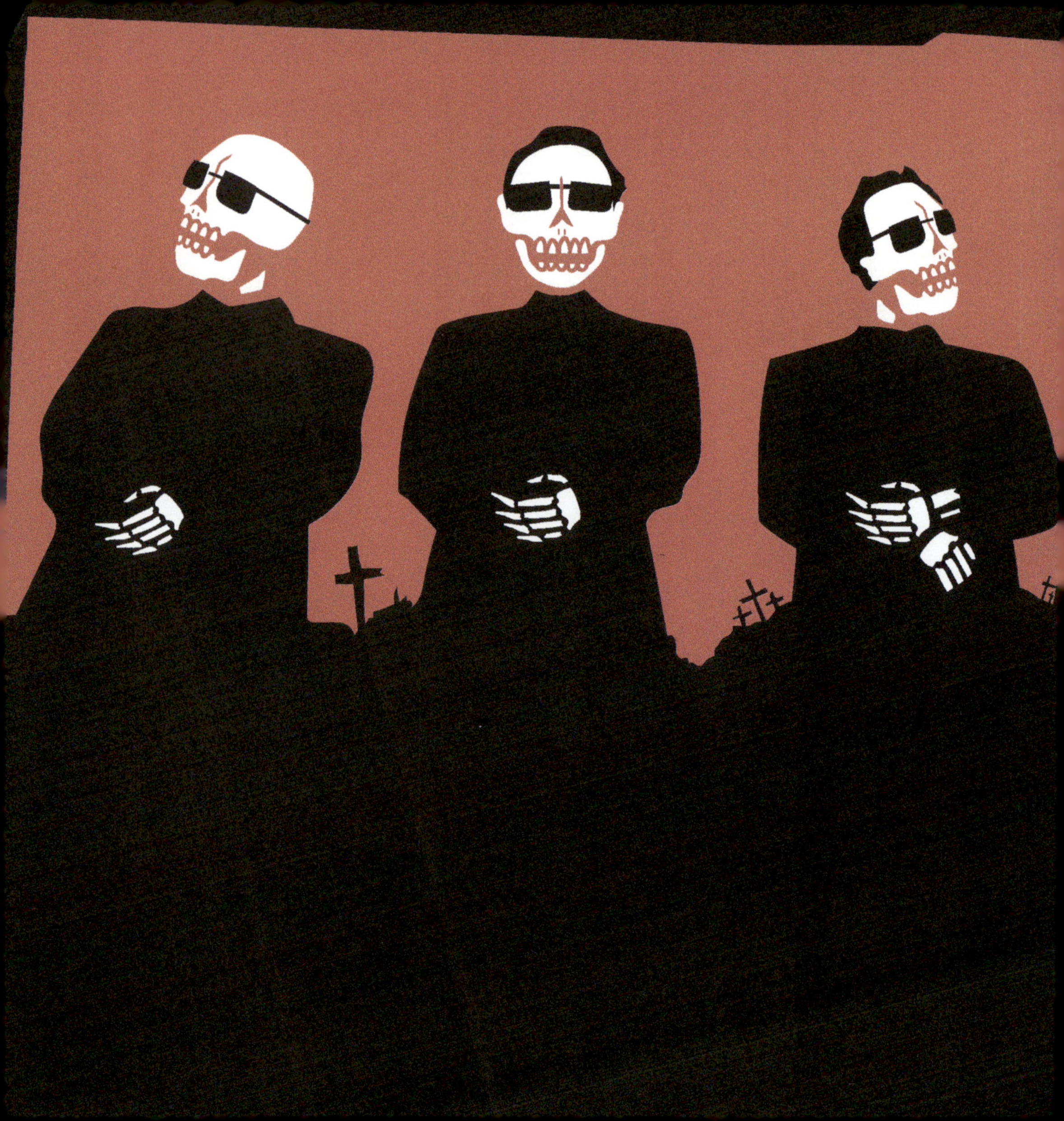

GOOD MOURNING
ALKALINE TRIO

Alkaline Trio showed that pop-punk could be poetic, dark, and captivating. Between Dan Andriano's love songs and Matt Skiba's macabre offerings, the contrasting tones make for a classic album that is equally cohesive and engaging.

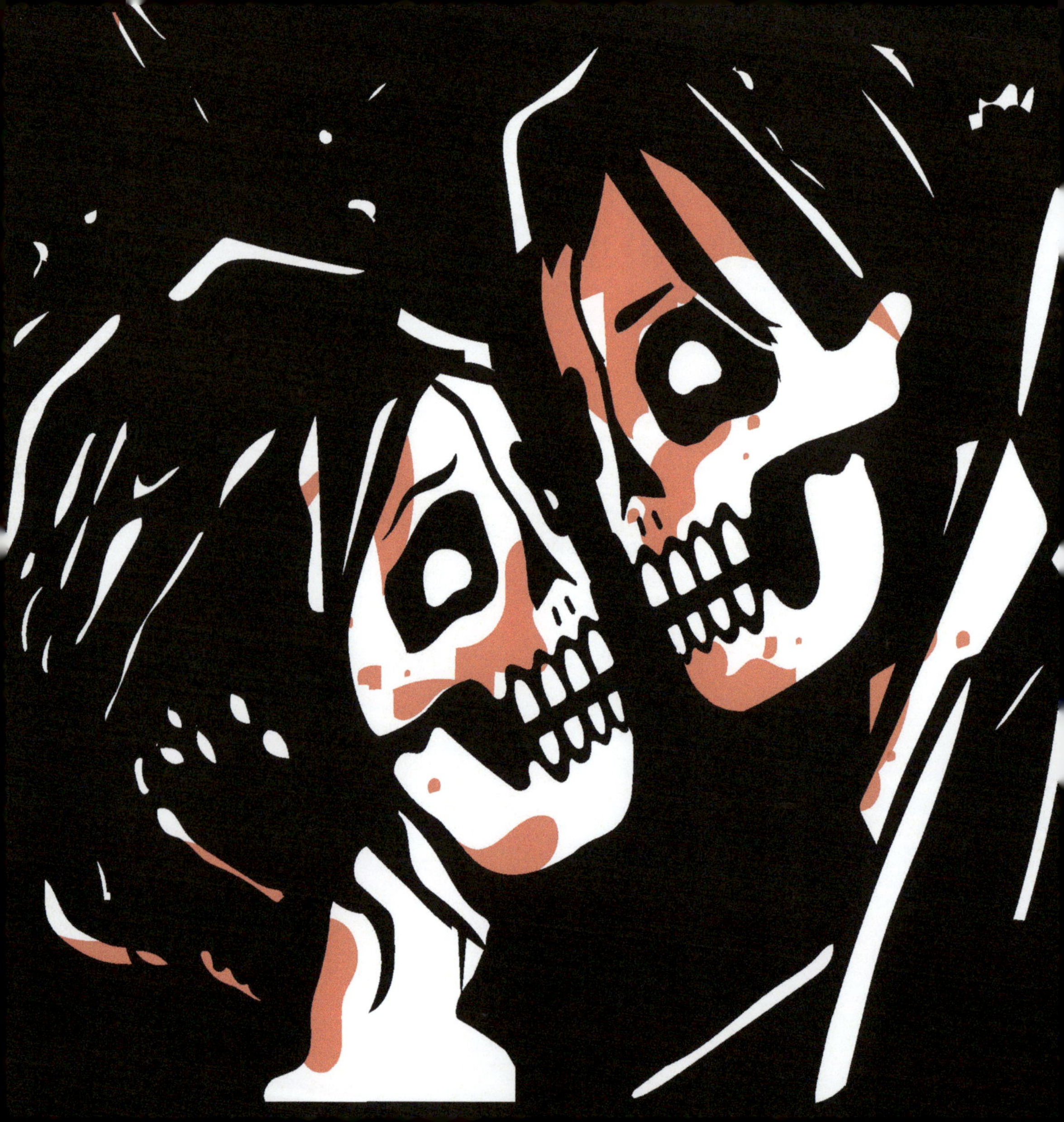

THREE CHEERS FOR SWEET REVENGE
MY CHEMICAL ROMANCE

One of the biggest releases commercially and historically, *Three Cheers For Sweet Revenge* put My Chemical Romance on the map. The album not only introduced new fans to this style of music, but also altered the course of the emo genre.

TELL ALL YOUR FRIENDS
TAKING BACK SUNDAY

Before becoming one of the biggest rock bands in North America, Taking Back Sunday was a small group from Long Island. This album changed everything for them. *Tell All Your Friends* helped redefine emo for that era and re-introduce the genre to the masses.

THE PLACES YOU'VE COME TO FEAR THE MOST
DASHBOARD CONFESSIONAL

The early work of Dashboard Confessional could all be considered "essential," but the stripped-down sincerity and heart-on-your-sleeve serenades of *The Places You've Come To Fear The Most* are a great starting point for emo music.

RIOT!
PARAMORE

If one record could be used to sum up the Warped Tour generation, *Riot!* by Paramore just may be that album. Blending alt-rock/emo, pop-punk, and guitar-driven pop rock, *Riot!* was an instant classic led by Hayley Williams and the Farro brothers.

STAY WHAT YOU ARE
SAVES THE DAY

One of the most revered emo bands, Saves The Day took a slight deviation on *Stay What You Are* at a time when its pop-punk peers were staying the course. There's no dishonesty in the experimentation here, just a marked maturity and refined sound.

SOMETHING TO WRITE HOME ABOUT
THE GET UP KIDS

The Vagrant Records era of emo/pop-punk provided the perfect soundtracks for many road trips. The seminal *Something To Write Home About* remains a timeless classic with driving choruses, catchy keyboards, and melodies that show the Get Up Kids in their finest hour.

BLEED AMERICAN
JIMMY EAT WORLD

Another crossover success story, *Bleed American* ruled mainstream alternative airwaves, and turned Jimmy Eat World from underdog emo heroes to rock-radio regulars. *Bleed American* showed off Jimmy Eat World's best; energetic arena alt-rock, ballads, and driving pop-punk/emo mid-tempo anthems.

ABOUT THE AUTHOR

Mike Damante is a journalist, award-winning educator and author.

Damante is the author of the non-fiction books "Punk Rock and UFOs: Stranger Than Fiction," "Punk Rock and UFOs: Cryptozoology meets Anarchy," and "Punk Rock and UFOs: True Believers," as well as the young adult fiction novel "Pumpkin Spice and Nothing Nice." He has appeared on various podcasts, radio shows and television programs. Damante wrote for his college newspaper, *The Daily Cougar,* at the University of Houston where he began covering music for their life and arts section. Damante also worked as a copy editor at the Houston Chronicle/Hearst Media. He currently produces a music/media blog MIKED for them. Damante has interviewed blink-182, Bad Religion, Alkaline Trio, Descendents, Aerosmith, B.o.B, Donald Glover, Interpol, New FoundGlory, Tegan and Sara, Angels & Airwaves, AFI, and others. He has covered multiple Warped Tours, and the X-Games.

ABOUT THE ARTIST

Cassie Podish is a Virginia-based designer/illustrator who mostly (but not exclusively) works in the music industry creating band merchandise, album covers, and more. She has worked with both major label artists and independent artists from all around the globe. While most of her clientele are musicians, labels, and bands, she is happy to work outside of that world and has created art for restaurants, clothing lines, and other businesses. Podish has worked with bands like Senses Fail, The Wonder Years, Circa Survive, Sum 41, Real Friends, Kevin Devine, Neck Deep, Seaway, Less Than Jake, and many more.